The
Transformation

EMERGING TO *New Life*

The
Transformation

EMERGING TO *New Life*

LAURA JAKA

Synergy Publishing
Newberry, FL 32669

Synergy Publishing
Newberry, FL 32669

The Transformation: Emerging to New Life
by Laura Jaka

Printed in the United States of America.

Library of Congress Catalog Card Number: 2021922997

International Standard Book Number: 978-1-61036-277-1

Editor, L. Edward Hazelbaker

Cover/Interior design by Kent Jensen | knail.com

BP 04/2022

DEDICATION

TO THE CHURCH'S Bridegroom, our beautiful love story is one that must be shared with the world. You are such a bridegroom that every bride should desire. You, Lord, faileth not!

Thank you for choosing me to be a part of your bride! I am in love with you more than I can express in words. I am immensely grateful to you, our sweet and faithful groom!

And to my dearest friend, the Holy Spirit, whose reverence and ministry has been abused by many for their own gain, while others have ignored you in fear of the undiluted truth of your ministry. Thank you for your humility and indispensable ministry on earth!

> *But when He, the Spirit of Truth, comes, He will guide you into all the truth [full and complete truth]. For He will not speak on His own initiative, but He will speak whatever He hears [from the Father—the message regarding the Son], and He will disclose to you what is to come [in the future].*   (John 16:13 AMP)

TABLE OF CONTENTS

INTRODUCTION

THE STORY YOU read in this book can be challenging. It will certainly challenge those who want to ignore the real but often unseen battle for souls that has continued unabated since the fall of man. That battle is not only real but also serious and a matter of life and death. And it's time for people to come to grips with it.

The enemy—the prince of the power of the air[1]—is still very much alive today. And perhaps he and his minions are more active today than ever before in both subtle and not-so-subtle ways, because they know the time of their freedom to hinder God's work is coming to an end.

But as challenged as you may become while reading my story, I hope you won't feel as uncomfortable or as challenged as I was while actually experiencing and dealing with all of it personally. But perhaps you are going through such a battle yourself. If you are, I hope my story in this book will be used by the Holy Spirit to encourage you to never give up the battle.

To help prepare you for reading my story of dealing with the enemy and undergoing many painful and confusing consequences because of it, please begin by not jumping to conclusions as you read. I am not attempting to make a doctrinal statement in this book. I am only telling you about what happened. You are free to form your own conclusions on doctrinal matters, but I assure you I am not lying or stretching the truth in my story.

---

1   Ephesians 2:2.

But if this book causes you to question your beliefs—regardless of whether they are based on how you have personally interpreted Scripture, or based just on what others have taught you—then so be it. And to resolve any matter in question concerning what you should or should not believe, I will only point you to the Bible and recommend you study all of it while at the same time praying for God to show you His Truth.

That is what I did. My experiences certainly drove me into God's Word. And they also drove me to pray more as I sought God for both deliverance from my enemies and grace to continue to grow in my knowledge of God and spiritual matters.

Finally, I will say only one more thing in the way of an introduction. And that is, I have already prayed for you. I asked God to somehow use my story in His plans to transform the life of anyone who reads it.

—Laura

CHAPTER 1

My Need of Transformation

Do not conform to the pattern of this world, but be transformed by the renewing of your mind. Then you will be able to test and approve what God's will is—his good, pleasing and perfect will.

(Romans 12:2)[2]

THINK ABOUT THE wonder of *Metamorphosis.*

A new life has been developing inside an egg that was deposited on the leaf of a plant. The egg splits open, and out crawls a little caterpillar. Well, that caterpillar is an eating machine. Over several weeks the caterpillar crawls around on its belly eating parts of every green leaf it can find.

The caterpillar eats and eats incessantly, and it grows larger and larger with each passing day. It stores away food like a

---

2 Unless otherwise noted, quoted Scriptures are from the New International Version.

veritable glutton. And as far as the caterpillar is concerned, there is nothing else to do. It's the only life it knows. Day after day passes. Week after week passes. And nothing much changes—except its size.

Then one day, the eating stops. The caterpillar knows that some kind of change is on the way. The type of life it has known is about to be over. A real challenge is ahead. Instinctively, the caterpillar attaches itself to a branch. And before long, the poor little caterpillar is encased in a close-fitting shell—called a chrysalis—that restricts its movement.

Its world has changed.

The caterpillar no longer has the freedom to crawl around on plants and eat itself silly. It has become a prisoner within its chrysalis. I can only wonder what goes on inside the mind of a caterpillar as it experiences such a dramatic event. Do you think it knows it is completely at the mercy of anyone who passes and sees it hanging there?

What a vulnerable and dangerous position to be in!

I can't help but wonder what it would be like to begin feeling my body beginning to undergo such dramatic and intense change. Is it lonely? Is it painful? To me it must be terrifying.

But perhaps the caterpillar simply sleeps through the whole ordeal. Or perhaps it just exists for a few weeks in some kind of stupefied state of mind until one day it wakes up, escapes its prison, stretches its new wings wide, and flies off into a new existence.

The lowly and basically fat, ugly, restricted caterpillar has become a trim, beautiful butterfly seemingly unfettered to fly away to explore and enjoy a new life of wonder.

As Creator, God determined to make the butterfly, and He chose the steps through which a butterfly develops and reproduces. God has a purpose for everything He does and for everything He allows to happen. And Scripture assures us that He continues to work through all the circumstances of life—the good and the bad—to bring about something good in the lives of all those who are called according to His purposes (Romans 8:28).

Metamorphosis is a Greek word meaning *transformation* or *change in shape.*

I have to believe that God wants us to learn something from the butterfly. At least I have. God has shown me through my own experiences that the ultimate power and creative genius it took to design the universe and determine the way of the butterfly is the same power we can depend on to transform our lives. And He is looking for opportunities to prove that to us every day.

I was born in 1976 in Freetown, Sierra Leone, West Africa. My mother, whom we call Adju, was very young when I was born, and in many ways she was unprepared to care for me. She depended on my grandmother, whom we called "Mamma," for most of my care and supervision.

Altogether, my mother gave birth to nine children. But not all of my brothers and sisters had the same father. I knew very little basically next to nothing—about what it could be like to live in a home and be raised by my parents. Most of my early life was spent in Mamma's home.

Mamma worked hard trying to take care of me and my siblings. But life itself was hard. She had little in the way of wealth and possessions, but she did her best for us. I always loved and appreciated Mamma. She did the best she could to provide for my needs, but my life was not what I would have liked, because my mother, Adju, was always in and out of it. And I had no real, meaningful relationship with my father.

I will leave out many details about my history as a young person, but I need to tell you that by the time I was five years old, I was being molested and raped multiple times by two men who lived not far from Mamma's house.

But that was only one of the experiences I had as a young person that affected how I viewed life.

As I grew older, the time eventually came when Mamma decided she no longer had what it took to care for us, so she reluctantly arranged for me to live with another relative. I had occasional contact with Mamma, my siblings, and my mother after that. But I never experienced what you could call a stable or normal family life, because anything that ever started to feel normal was soon disrupted by one thing or another.

My father suddenly came back into my life for a time, and I had an opportunity to go live with him in Italy. So I moved to Italy at the age of fourteen and lived with him and his wife. I managed to work multiple jobs in Italy as an underage worker while still in middle school. From that early age I was demonstrating considerable initiative and a willingness to work hard to help meet my family's needs.

But eventually my father left Italy and returned to Africa. I stayed in Italy, though, and continued my education. But I did not do so well because of all the things going on in my mind. I wasn't applying myself as I should. I barely passed middle school, and then I quit school altogether.

Amazingly, after I worked in Italy for several years, one of my bosses arranged for me to travel to the United States, and he spent money to help me get my travel authorization. I arrived in America a few months short of my twentieth birthday. After arriving in America I first stayed with my initial host family—a family related to the girlfriend of one of my brothers.

My host family consisted of both a father and mother who had two small children—a boy and a girl. Living with them gave me my first experience with a truly "normal" nuclear family. I felt privileged to have the opportunity.

I stayed in their home and cared for both of the children for the first few months in America, but I eventually started working. And in time I left my host home and moved into an apartment with some of my coworkers.

For time's sake I must skip a lot of details. I'll merely say that a lot of things transpired in the ensuing years. I moved several times before finally being able to settle down and establish roots in one location. I gained a lot of work experience and proved that I could be trusted to do well in just about any work or profession to which I applied myself.

But I also made a lot of bad decisions.

I allowed myself to form relationships with people who later disappointed me or caused me grief. I got into relationships with men who seemed to be loving and respectful but later proved to be cheaters, lazy, and abusive. I have to admit that I seemed to gravitate toward men who abused me. It was as if I was actually foolish enough to think there was some kind of value to be found in allowing men to continue to abuse and take advantage of me.

I became pregnant in time, and I let my boyfriend convince me I should get an abortion. I deeply regret having the abortion. Clearly, my life was not on the right path.

I do have one success story, though. One of my friends encouraged me to take a placement exam at a local university.

Remember, I had not been educated beyond middle school. But I passed the exam and was admitted to the school. It wasn't easy to juggle my education and work, but I eventually graduated with a high grade point average and degree in Sociology with a minor in Criminal Justice.

But I still was not always making good decisions, and as I walked across the stage to receive my diploma, if a person were to notice, a slight bulge under my graduation gown could reveal to them I was expecting another child.

My daughter, Camilla, was born in March of 2004. I have done everything I can to make sure she does not experience life without her mother. She is my joy, and I will do what I can to make sure her life is different from my early life.

I worked hard to support Camilla and also help support my family in Africa, and I continue to do that even now. I eventually married and was able to give a father to Camilla. But after a time I was once again disappointed by a man, and once again it was just Camilla and me.

But I know that even with all the problems, all the bad decisions, and all the challenging situations we have found ourselves in, God has been mindful of them all. I have not always faithfully followed His plan for my life, but He has always been faithful in loving me and continuing to hold out His hand to me. His love and concern for us are without measure. They are unfathomable. And they are very real.

Now I have written for you a few words to reveal to you the theme of this book. And I have provided to you some background about my life. You should understand by now that for many years

I was living a life that desperately needed to be transformed by the only One who has the power to do it—Jesus.

I know that now better than I ever have in the past.

I have long believed in God. I was raised in Catholicism, and my grandmother prayed to God. That was a good influence on me. And I grew up believing in God. But so did so many others who mistreated me, and that caused confusion in my life.

The fact is, I knew something about God's love for us. But knowing *about* Him and attending mass to hear more *about* Him did not automatically translate into me *knowing* Him. It was a long time before I came to really know Him. And in this book you will find out more about that.

Also, knowing about God did not mean that I knew much about *living for Him*. But I can now say that I have a personal relationship with God, and I'm not only intent on knowing Him better but also determined to live for Him and help others know Him too.

I began considering what God wanted of me and grew in my prayer life after my daughter was born. With all that was within me, I wanted to be a good mother. I wanted to provide my daughter with relationships and stability that I never had. And deep down I knew those would never be possible without God doing something more in my life and family.

But there is one other thing I need to relate to you before I tell you the story of my transformation into not only a genuine, active believer but also a *follower* of God.

From a young age I have been a person who dreams often. And while I will not say that all my dreams have been from God— that is, God was not always showing me things in dreams that He wanted me to know—enough of my dreams have been confirmed to me by events that followed that I know God has been trying to involve himself in my life for a very long time.

God has been trying to transform my life and my relationship with Jesus Christ for much longer than I have actually lived to please and know Him.

That is humbling to me, and I can't adequately express how that motivates me today.

What you are about to read did not take place before I determined in my heart to follow God. I determined to know Him and follow Him first. And as I look at it now, that level of belief and determination was the key to releasing the Holy Spirit to take the battle for my soul and the future of my daughter to the enemy.

Spiritual battles are real, and sometimes the enemy's reach is such that only Christ can fully fathom it. Sometimes only Jesus can understand the depth of confusion on the spiritual battlefield, because He has been in the battle for a long time. And it is He, himself, who cuts through the confusion and leads Heaven's host in the battle for our lives.

CHAPTER 2

The Beginning of Troubling Things

Be alert and of sober mind. Your enemy the devil prowls around like a roaring lion looking for someone to devour. (1 Peter 5:8)

IT ALL STARTED on December 31, 2018, the last day of the year—the day that can bring both joy and sadness at the same time depending on what transpired throughout the previous three hundred and sixty-five days. But to me, it was a day to celebrate with gratitude for all God had done for my daughter and me. And I planned on celebrating.

As I would so often do before going to an event, I went shopping. I found myself a beautiful white dress coat. It was customary for me to wear white on the last day of the year. I paired my white dress coat with a pair of silver high heels. I had gotten my hair done the previous week. So after shopping I was ready to ring in the New Year in style.

It was time for me to get ready, and my daughter was in the room with me as we discussed my outfit. She was giving me tips on how to make sure I was well coordinated. It was one of those daughter-mother moments that I cherish. In the end, I asked her to take some pictures of me, which she did. The pictures turned out so well that we both marveled at how beautiful I looked.

I'm smiling as I write this, because it turned out to be a not-so-beautiful day that will remain in our memories for the rest of our lives.

We both sat on my bed shortly after the pictures were taken and watched something on the TV as I waited a while before leaving the house for the party I was attending. While sitting on the bed, I began to feel a strange crawling sensation on the head. I ignored it at first, kept watching TV, and continued my conversation with my daughter. However, the feeling continued, so I asked my daughter to examine my head.

She did that and saw nothing. The feeling, though, continued. I asked my daughter to look again, for the crawling sensation was getting a bit more pronounced. Her response was the same as the first time. Still yet, I continued to feel the crawling sensation on my head. But not knowing what to make of it, we continued on with what we were doing.

I had dreamed many dreams over the years. And a friend (with whom I am no longer friends) had introduced me to a middle-aged woman who she said could interpret dreams. My friend told me the person was a co-worker of hers and expressed her trust in her ability to reveal the meanings of dreams.

I know now that I shouldn't have done it, but I began to share my dreams with the woman, and she then provided me with interpretations and instructions pertaining to my dreams. I felt my dreams were important, so I followed every instruction the woman gave me without second-guessing the validity of the source. I simply trusted my friend's recommendation.

Eventually, I realized the dreams that most puzzled and bothered me began to happen shortly after my return from my birthplace of Freetown, Sierra Leone, where I had gone to attend my late uncle's funeral a few months earlier in August of 2018.

Prior to my trip to Freetown, I received all of my vaccines here in the States and adhered to all precautionary measures while in Freetown. But even with all of that, I became very sick when I returned to the United States. The illness actually started on the airplane on my way back to the States.

While in Freetown, I experienced an upset stomach now and then, which wasn't anything that caused me to panic. I had also lost some weight. But nothing seemed all that far out of the ordinary, because I had experienced similar things during previous visits. Nonetheless, as a precaution I went to my doctor, who evaluated me and prescribed something to counter whatever virus she assumed had attacked me. I took the medications as prescribed and recovered well.

Or did I? What followed was a series of events that I in no way could understand.

———

I ended up not going out to the New Year's Eve party even after all my preparations. Something just didn't seem right. So I lay down and slept. And I didn't think much about the crawling sensation after that night because it appeared to have subsided.

I looked forward to the New Year. However, it turned out to be something I could have never imagined.

When I went back to work after the holidays, the crawling started again. And it became a constant event that would not go away. It became very frustrating. I could feel the movement on my head but could not physically feel anything there when I touched my head.

I took out my hair extensions—thinking I was experiencing an allergic reaction from them. But the hair extensions had nothing to do with it, and the crawling intensified. I became increasingly restless. Meanwhile, I continued to dream, and the so-called dream interpreter interpreted my dreams and gave me instructions that I obeyed.

On one occasion, I dreamed of a snake-like figure resting on my dining table. I shared the dream with the dream interpreter. But unlike on previous occasions when she shared with me what she thought my dreams meant, she didn't attempt to explain that one. At the time, I was ignorant of what I should expect from her, so I didn't press her for an interpretation.

God has always known about how in our ignorance we are apt to listen to the wrong counsel and choose destructive paths. He breathed words through the Holy Spirit to the prophet Hosea for him to deliver to the people. Part of Hosea 4:6 says, *"My people are destroyed from lack of knowledge"* (KJV).

The Israelites had gotten themselves into a lot of trouble because of their lack of knowledge, and because of my own lack of knowledge of the Word of God, I certainly was not prepared for that season of my life.

Truthfully, I thought I knew the Bible well enough, because I had read and studied it over the years. But clearly, I still lacked much knowledge, and there were many things I still didn't understand. I hadn't a clue of how deficient I was in the whole counsel of the Word of God. And there was a price to pay for my ignorance. But God not only knew of my ignorance of the Word, He also continued to extended to me His grace as He continued to work in my life.

Eventually my dreams became stranger and stranger and began to come to me at an alarming rate. On several occasions I dreamed of snakes appearing in different scenarios. Once, I dreamed of a snake resting on my left cheek, but I wasn't bitten or hurt.

The most vivid of all those dreams, though, was when I saw a white horse standing on my front lawn. I noticed that the horse looked at me, but there wasn't any interaction between us, and that was the end of it.

One morning, as was customary for me, I spent time in devotion before leaving for work. I was listening to a gospel message with a cup of coffee in my hand. Suddenly, I became very sleepy. I laid aside my coffee mug to lie down. And as I lay down, I was no longer completely alert but found myself in what I would call a trance episode.

During that episode I could hear and feel everything that was happening, but yet I was in more of a semi-conscious state. I saw a black plastic trash bag like those heavy-duty trash bags used to dispose of heavy trash. From within the bag, a big, dark-black hand rose up to display an arm from its elbow up. I knew it had power. And as the hand raised from within the bag, I heard what seemed like something moaning or crying in distress.

I saw other things at the time that I won't relate now, and they all confused me. But I will say that at the end I saw a very tall man with the physique of my late uncle, Kofi, standing in the room. He looked at me, said, "Laura, I am leaving," and walked out of the room.

In my trance, or vision, I then walked into the bathroom adjacent to where he stood, and there before me was what appeared to be his military uniform left on the floor (my late uncle, who died over thirty years ago, was in the army). I picked up his uniform and hung it on the bathroom door. I also took his military boots and positioned them next to his uniform.

I became completely conscious at that point. The entire episode happened in less than twenty minutes. And after it was over, I lay in bed for a while perplexed about the meaning. I then regained my composure, prayed, and left for work.

As best I could, I continued on with life as usual not knowing what to make of all the happenings. And thankfully, I had a devotional life to the extent that I knew how to pray, praise, and worship God, which is what my daughter and I did. One night after praying with my daughter, she left for her bedroom, and I lay on my bed and continued to talk with God.

As I prayed, I silently pled for God to give me a sense of insight into all that was happening around and to us.

Then, as unexpectedly as the earlier trance event came upon me, I had another type of experience. Both of my eyes were wide open, and I saw what looked like an octopus' head with several of what looked like snake-like figures dancing or wriggling on top of the big octopus' head. Now that was not like a trance. I was fully aware and awake, and it seemed like something that was physically before me.

I lay motionless in bed and asked God for an explanation. But I received no answer. Then I thought of a Scripture.

He will cover you with his feathers, and under his wings you will take refuge; his faithfulness will be your shield and rampart. You will not fear the terror of the night, nor the arrow that flies by day. (Psalm 91:4-5)

I watched the creature wriggle and twist in front of me. Then, two of the snake-like things flew off from the big octopus' head and flew above me. At that point, I got up and went into my daughter's room and asked her to come sleep with me. I didn't want to sleep alone.

My daughter and I lay down together on the bed that night trusting what David so pointedly wrote in Psalm 143:8. *"Let the morning bring me word of your unfailing love, for I have put my trust in you."*

We slept in peace without incident and without concern about what I had seen. I had no understanding of the meaning of the things I was experiencing, but I continued to place my trust in God.

CHAPTER 3

Seeking a Solution

Consider and hear me, O LORD my God; enlighten my eyes, lest I sleep the sleep of death; lest my enemy say, "I have prevailed against him"; lest those who trouble me rejoice when I am moved.
(Psalm 13:3-4 NKJV)

SHORTLY AFTER THE incident of seeing the octopus with the snake-like appendages on top of its head, I was in the parking lot of a shopping center when I believed I heard in my spirit that I should write to a prominent pastor. I felt like I should visit his church and share my experiences with him.

I went into *Instagram* and sent a private message to him since it was the only way I knew how to reach him. I monitored my *Instagram* account for a response for days, but there was none. I then asked my friend whom I call my sister-friend—because she has become my dear sister-in-Christ—to visit his church with me. I didn't want my daughter and me to go alone. My friend decided to bring her son, too, and we made plans to attend the following Sunday.

The pastor's church is out of state (a megachurch known around the world), so we had to drive there the night before and stay in a hotel. Before leaving, though, I printed the message I had written to him on *Instagram* in hopes of there being a way for him to read my message in case he hadn't gotten to it.

After spending the night in the hotel, we got up early that Sunday morning and attended part of the 8:30 AM service. Then we also stayed for the 11:00 AM service. I had given the written message to the church's security team when we arrived and asked them to please make sure the pastor received it.

When the pastor made an altar call toward the end of the second service, I raced down the altar, pulling my daughter behind me. We were the first people to reach the front. And I was able to talk with the pastor briefly as he extended his hand to greet me. I shared that I had driven from Georgia and believed the Lord had asked me to come see him.

He pointed me to a door and asked me to follow the rest of the people who responded to the altar call. I did as he instructed. We entered a large room and met with several people who were waiting to talk with us and provide us with information about the church.

I waited patiently for the pastor to join me, but instead, he sent an elder of the church to talk with me. He was an older gentleman who was very nice. He introduced himself and asked for my reason for wanting to see the pastor. I shared with him briefly about me and shared what I had seen both in visions and dreams. I told him that I believed God had asked me to come there and meet with his pastor.

The man then left after saying to me, "Wait here."

I thought we were still waiting for the pastor to come and meet us. But to the contrary, the man returned with a middle-aged African couple—husband and wife—and a young African-American woman. So the team then present with us was comprised of the older gentleman, the African couple, and the young African-American woman—whose actual role at the church I don't remember.

They prayed for us again, and then the man said, "I brought the African couple because they would understand what you shared with me more than I would." The African couple prayed for us again before the wife decided to admonish me. After praying, she said to me, "You must not dabble in two worlds."

She continued, "You have to let go of one and serve only God."

"Dabble in two worlds?" I was offended! You mean to tell me that I drove hours, spent the night in a hotel, came to the church seeking help, and I'm told I must not dabble in two worlds? "What was she missing?" I asked myself. "What is it about the information I shared with them that caused her to form such a conclusion?"

I defended myself politely by saying, "I only *dabble* in God's world, and I've never dabbled in two worlds."

Both the older gentleman and the African-American lady had already left my daughter and me with the African couple. And after the wife's reprimand, there was really not much else I could say to her, so I expressed my gratitude, and we said our goodbyes.

I reconnected with my friend and her son, who had been in the lobby waiting for us. Then we made the drive back to Georgia, arriving late in the evening. Throughout the following week, I called members of that church for prayers as I was instructed by the church's team of counselors, but I could not get any of them to answer the phone—even with several attempts to reach them.

However, I never bothered to attempt to call the African couple, because I knew the wife's opinion of me. Surprisingly, though, the African-American lady actually called me days later for a brief follow up. And that turned out to be my last interaction with members of that church.

I was particularly hurt by that experience, because after sincerely attempting to follow what I believed God wanted me to do—seek out a man of God in the person of that pastor for counsel—I felt his response turned out to be something like I would expect to receive from some celebrity who was largely disconnected from my needs.

But could I have been wrong about God's prompting? I admit that's possible since I know I lacked proper understanding to discern many things at the time.

However, I was determined to continue to gain more knowledge in spiritual things. So I continued seeking God and trusting Him to supply my needs and answers to my many questions. I was clearly disappointed in my experience with that church—and especially after they did not honor their offer of follow-up opportunities for prayers with me. But I decided to chalk it up to a learning experience.

As time went on, there was no real change to what we were experiencing, but we kept praying and relying on God. I began spending a lot of time in the guest room in our home. One day, I was in the room lying down, covered with a blanket and watching TV, when suddenly I felt like something was crawling on my legs.

By then I actually had come to the place where I expected to experience troubling things. But that still bothered me. So I pulled the blanket off my legs and shook it. As I did that, I saw one of the snake-like things that I had seen flying off the octopus' head. It flew off the blanket into the air and disappeared.

I got up, folded the blanket, and put it away. Then I went back to watching TV. At this point you are probably asking, "What was she thinking?"

Here's my answer:

Have I not commanded you? Be strong and courageous. Do not be afraid; do not be discouraged, for the LORD your God will be with you wherever you go. (Joshua 1:9)

God was assuring Joshua of His protection as Joshua assumed the role of leading the Israelites into the promise land. I took hold of God's assurance to Joshua. And I continue to apply it to my daughter and me wherever we may be. If Joshua could put His confidence in God to be with him, so can we. God is the same yesterday, today, and forever.[3]

I am by no means implying that I was no longer concerned about my experiences at that point. To the contrary, I was becoming more and more concerned. But instead of being a coward and living in fear, I was determined to trust in the Lord as I continued to wonder about the origin of the creature I saw and its insistence on wanting to be around me.

Following that experience I was praying one afternoon at work after having implemented a more intense prayer schedule

---

3   Hebrews 13:8.

throughout the day. I was not just praying in the morning and before bed. So on that day as I prayed quietly in my heart, I heard this word burst into my mind: "Blanket." I immediately left work and rushed home. I knew I needed to dispose of the blanket.

On my way home I called my friend to join me. By the favor of God, she was available, and I shared with her my intention. She was more than willing to help me. We arrived at my home and retrieved the blanket. But before disposing of it, we prayed.

As we prayed I was surprised to hear my friend begin to pray in tongues. Showing my surprise, I asked, "You speak in tongues?"

She only smiled.

I felt then that my friend must know something about what was at stake with me. But I hadn't shared anything with her, nor had she been privy to all that had happened. She knew nothing except that I called and said I needed her support.

Before then, I had learned that when a person prays in tongues, he or she is tapping into the inner man and concealing the prayer from the enemy, since only God understands what the person is praying. I was a bit troubled at that point. "What does this all mean?" I quietly asked myself.

After we finished disposing of the blanket, I thanked her, and we said our goodbyes. I felt like something had been resolved in my situation. But in time I found out that dealing with the blanket was only a small beginning toward solving the mystery behind my experiences.

I will tell you now about another experience I had in the following month of May 2019. I was fully awake during that experience. I stood watching what looked like a movie playing in front of me.

I once again saw a white horse, and it became apparent that it was the same white horse I had seen before. I then saw a frame of a woman who actually looked like me. Then I saw a man dressed in a suit—then two children, a boy, and a girl. Then, finally, I could see the full picture of a family in a park setting with the children playing on a swing. It appeared, though, that a woman was lying flat on a surface within the family's image that had been painted before me.

As I continued to look, there appeared before me what looked like the face of Jesus. Then to my amazement there appeared an image of the face of Mary, the Blessed Mother of Jesus. I looked yet again and saw what looked like a bouquet of white flowers lying to the right side of the perfect picture that seemed to have actually been painted on canvas before my eyes.

Earlier in the day, I had taken some flowers to my church (my Catholic church) and placed a bouquet by the statue of the Blessed Mary, another by Saint Joseph's statue, and another by the statue of Jesus. It was customary for people to bring flowers and place them on those statues at any time they chose, so I did it that day.

Then, as I continued to behold the scene before me, to my amazement I began to feel someone standing behind me engraving something with a piercing sting on my left shoulder. I did not turn around though, and as the feeling continued, I began to see what looked like a lion in the middle of the already completed family picture.

My focus then changed to what was being engraved on my left shoulder blade. The sting began to hurt. It felt like a sharp instrument was being used to carve the sign or what felt like the letter S. Curious, I turned around to look, and it seemed that whatever it was that was hurting me quickly made a jump away from behind me so that I did not see who or what it was.

That episode continued to affect me for several hours into the night. I became exhausted in my mind from dealing with it, so I prayed this simple prayer:

> Lord, I thank you for visiting me and showing me the picture of the family you have prepared for me. I thank you, Jesus, and Blessed Mary, for visiting me. Lord, I am now tired, so I am going to bed. Please forgive me for not being able to stay awake to allow you to continue.

But before actually going to bed, I called the dream interpreter to share what I had seen. (Yes, I was still involved with her.) I was sure she would be interested to know that the white horse had once again appeared to me. I attempted to call her several times, but she didn't answer her phone. However, I was still eager to tell what had occurred, so I called again the following morning, and I was able to share the story.

But the response I received from the dream interpreter set off an alarm bell in my mind. Her response was, "You'll continue to see more."

For some reason, because of that statement, something didn't feel right in my spirit, and I then thought to myself, "Whose voice are you listening to, God's voice or the enemy's?"

I began wondering if God wasn't the only one trying to speak to me or affect my life and thoughts. Here is what the Apostle Paul wrote to the Corinthian Christians:

> *But I will continue doing what I have always done. This will undercut those who are looking for an opportunity to boast that their work is just like ours. These people are false apostles. They*

are deceitful workers who disguise themselves as apostles of Christ. But I am not surprised! Even Satan disguises himself as an angel of light. (2 Corinthians 11:12-14 NLT)

I wondered if I had fallen victim to someone like those the Apostle Paul wrote about. Sadly, though, I could not tell, because the dream interpreter seemed genuine to me, and she displayed an attitude that projected to me a sense of calm.

There was one thing that I especially noticed and started thinking about during that period of time. It seemed the more I was engaged in pursuing God and gaining spiritual understanding, the stranger the incidents I experienced became. So I wondered what that could mean, because many things were still not becoming clear to me. If anything, I was becoming more confused by them and felt the need for more answers.

One afternoon, I was standing fully engaged in what I was doing when I began to feel a wrapping sensation on my face. It was as if something substantially heavy was caressing itself all over my face. I could feel it, but like when feeling some other things on me, nothing was visible. There were no visible signs or any physical marks on my face. Amazed at what was happening, I became motionless and frozen in place.

With no way for me to identify such strange experiences, I just continued to pray and depend on God to be in control. Paul wrote, *"But whenever anyone turns to the Lord, the veil is taken away"* (2 Corinthians 3:16). Most certainly, I needed a veil removed from my understanding, so I continued to press in further with God.

However, it seemed like He was absent. Of course He wasn't—something I knew to be the truth. But I finally came to realize that I had been unfaithful to God by trusting in another source for guidance. And that had, in effect, developed into an idolatrous relationship.

So it was my own choices that caused Him to remain in the background, but I still knew He had not abandoned me. And what happened next was used by God to prove to me He was with me in the midst of the storm.

There was an earthquake in Georgia one night that seemingly shook everyone except me. I slept through the entire night and didn't realize what had taken place until late the next afternoon—when I realized that my backyard had been affected. After coming home from work, as I stood in the kitchen looking out the window, I saw that four of my very tall pine trees with massive roots had fallen into my neighbor's yard, breaking our shared fence.

Then the Holy Spirit impressed on my heart that the Lord had intervened and interrupted something on my behalf to protect our house.

I then separated myself from the counsel of the dream interpreter. And after having the Holy Spirit confirm God's love and concern to me, I felt a sense of normalcy could finally return to my and my daughter's lives.

But my anticipation of a fresh start for us was short lived.

CHAPTER 4

A New Appeal for Help

Help me, Lord my God; save me according to your unfailing love. (Psalm 109:26)

I DECIDED MY daughter and I would hold a twelve-hour fast from midnight to noon one day as I continued my quest to be closer to God. And I hoped He would bring things to light and help me understand the things we were experiencing.

I had been to the hospital emergency room on several occasions with breathing problems and chest pains. After proper medical evaluation, though, all tests yielded negative results regarding any life-threatening condition. So I wasn't concerned about going through the fast with my daughter.

During our fast, we took turns praying throughout the morning hours. Around 6:00 AM the Lord spoke to me and said,

"Anoint yourself," which I did. But I didn't only anoint myself; I woke up my daughter and anointed her too. I then went back to lie down, and I continued to pray periodically before our scheduled time to break our fast.

Around noon, as we were getting ready to break our fast, I felt something forcefully wrapping itself around my neck with such pressure that it felt like I was being choked. My daughter was in another room. Thankfully, I was able to call out to her from where I was.

As she walked in where I was, I said to her, "I can't breathe!"

That was all I remember before passing out and falling to the floor.

I woke up shortly thereafter with these words in my mouth: "He that's in me is greater than he that's in the world" (from 1 John 4:4). And I repeated those words over and over as I stood up and paced the hallway. I had no idea how those words were impressed in my heart but they certainly were. It had to have been God!

A big lump developed on my forehead because I hit my head on a nightstand when I fell. And I had a pounding headache by the time I heard sirens blazing through my subdivision. My daughter had called 911 when I passed out.

When the firefighters and paramedics arrived, they insisted on taking me in an ambulance to the hospital. Even though I didn't fully understand it all at the time, I knew I had suffered an attack from the enemy, so I hesitated to go to the hospital. But I eventually agreed to go, because they really would have it no other way due to my head injury.

At the emergency room I was assigned a male nurse who is from Africa. When he came into my room, he said, "When you came in, I looked at you and said, 'she's not an ordinary person.'"

He then continued, "The enemy came to scare you."

His first statement about me not being an ordinary person did not really surprise me, because I had heard it said to me before on a few other occasions. But his second statement did.

Several thoughts passed through my mind, like, "Why would the enemy come to scare me?"

"What did I do to the enemy that caused him to attack me?"

"Which roads have I traveled that served to prepare his way for his attack?"

"How has my disobedience to the Word of God opened a door to make my daughter or me vulnerable to the enemy's attack?"

"What have I done either knowingly or unknowingly that positioned my daughter and me to become targets of his attacks?"

I was full of conflicted thoughts and emotions while trying to dissect the nurse's comments.

The doctor walked into the room as I still pondered those thoughts. She examined me and suggested that I should be admitted for observation—not only because I had hit my head but also because of my prior visits to the hospital with complaints of chest pains and difficulty breathing.

She was a doctor whom I sensed had a feeling of extra concern for my daughter and me. The doctor became even more alarmed after I shared that my daughter and I lived alone at home. At that, she told me she would consult with my cardiologist, and then she left the room. (Because of those earlier symptoms, I had been under the supervision of a cardiologist.)

My daughter was sitting next to me, and she was visibly dismayed over all that was happening. And after hearing what the doctor said, my daughter immediately jumped on the bed and said, "Mommy, let's pray!"

Throughout our lives we have known that God is good! He had always been our constant help. So in a moment of need, such as we were then facing, Camilla suggested that we resort to what we knew to do: Pray!

David, whom God himself recognized as a man after His own heart,[4] knew who to turn to in his time of need. David wrote, *"Because you are my helper, I sing for joy in the shadow of your wings. I cling to you; your strong right hand holds me securely"* (Psalm 63:7-8 NLT).

It's such a joy to know that my daughter is growing into a woman with a similar heart toward dependency on God and a desire to honor Him at all times.

And unbeknownst to me, Camilla had familiarized herself with the room and spotted a Bible resting on a shelf. She grabbed the Bible and opened it to Psalm 91. I immediately burst into tears, because I knew whatever the outcome, her hope and trust was centered on the God who could turn it all around.

We both read the Psalm and trusted in God.

A short time later, I decided to leave the hospital. It was contrary to what the doctor had advised, but I signed myself out and asked a friend to pick us up. We stayed at her place for the rest of the weekend, and it was there where I soon found myself in deep contemplation.

I had distanced myself from the dream interpreter because I was convinced I had trespassed on dangerous territory. And I became determined that it was best in the future to keep the full details of events to myself and only rely on God for directions. With that in my mind, my daughter and I began spending the

---

4 "After removing Saul, he made David their king. God testified concerning him: 'I have found David son of Jesse, a man after my own heart; he will do everything I want him to do'" (Acts 13:22).

night at the friend's place more often than we actually intended, but I knew we needed to be around other people.

I also developed a routine to follow while my daughter was at school. I spent most of each day at the Adoration Chapel at our Catholic church worshiping and seeking more of God. Everything about my life changed at that point. Both my work life and my personal life became non-existent. I could not function by any means. My thought processes were derailed. My mind was no longer my own. I could not seem to make sense of who I was or what I should be doing day after day.

The only thing that made sense to me—that felt natural and normal—was to be in the presence of God. So I began attending 9:00 AM Mass. Then immediately afterward I sat in the Adoration Chapel until around 3:00 PM, when it was almost time for my daughter to come home from school. That became my regular schedule five days a week.

A particular fear was introduced into my life after the attack that put me in the hospital, and it played a significant role in my thought process. However, something else was introduced to me as well, and that was a seemingly insatiable and genuine hunger for God.

Prior to the start of all those events that changed me so, I had been planning for my mother to relocate here from Freetown, Sierra Leone. But her visa approval had been a difficult process. According to U.S. Citizenship and Immigration Services requirements for filing for a parent, I was well qualified as a naturalized citizen of the United States. And I could financially provide for my mother. But none of that seemed to matter. So I sought help from my senator's office.

Shortly after I filed a request with the senator's office, my mother's visa was approved. I made arrangements for her to be with us within a week. My daughter and I were elated. Camilla was finally going to meet her grandmother for the first time in her life. And I was eager to continue building a bond with my mother that I never had due to our fractured relationship that existed during all of my childhood.

We felt blessed. But we could not have realized what lie ahead of us. Absolutely nothing could have prepared my daughter and me for what would transpire after my mother came to live with us.

I celebrated my forty-third birthday a few days before my mother's arrival. Actually, there was no physical celebration. But I was grateful to have lived to see the day after all I had been through. Camilla and I were once again living in our own home, and I was away from work for a while so my mother and I could spend some time catching up.

Everything seemed normal as far as having her living with us. My mother was adjusting well to life in America. I shared with my mother our recent plight and how I had spent much of my time at the Adoration Chapel. And my mother began to join me in my spiritual routine. She attended church with us on Sunday and joined me at 9:00 AM Mass almost daily on weekdays.

I told my mother that the routine seemed normal to me at that point in my life. Going to church, spending time in the Adoration Chapel, praying, and fasting all just made sense to me. And frankly, not much else did anymore.

I had been a Catholic since growing up in Italy, so I became accustomed to the ways of *doing* church. But for what we were facing I knew I was going to need more of *Jesus*—not merely a church.

I could not connect the dots of what was happening at first, but I eventually realized even stranger things were beginning to happen in our lives, and they seemed to coincide with my mother's arrival to live with us

Without a doubt, I knew I had crossed a wrong path by getting involved with the dream interpreter. And as I continued to put pieces together I came to realize that going home to Freetown to attend my uncle's funeral in 2018 had attracted something strange to my life. But an additional mystery was soon added to the already complicated matters that seemed to engulf our lives.

While struggling with it all, I received a call and was told that my best friend, who was living in Virginia, had been hit and killed by a car. I wondered how I could handle such tragedy while already dealing with where life had taken my daughter and me. But I knew we had to respond to what was happening the best we could.

I knew that if the situation were reversed, my friend would have without hesitation taken on the responsibility and role of being a mother to my daughter if she needed her. So despite my situation and feelings at the time, I knew her own teenage daughter she left behind needed me. So I gathered myself and pushed through that painful loss that we were all suffering, made arrangements, and drove to Virginia with my daughter and mother.

I shared with my mother much of what had occurred in my life in the previous year, and of course my daughter was fully aware of all of it. But there was one thing that neither of them knew about—the suicidal thoughts I was then wrestling with. There was this constant voice telling me to kill myself. It was very real and always present, so I began to entertain those thoughts and wondered if I would indeed be better off dead.

But by God's grace, He allowed the Holy Spirit's voice to speak louder to me, and my thinking began shifting to thoughts of my daughter not having a mother. That, coupled with my concern that I might sin against God if I were to take my own life, was important in pulling me through. But even with those things considered, I know that, ultimately, I can only credit my decision to survive and press on to the power of God.

While still dealing with suicidal thoughts at the time, I hid them from everyone and fully engaged myself in the planning of my best friend's funeral. I look now at some of the pictures that were taken the day of her funeral and wonder how I was able to mask what was then my reality. In the pictures, everything appeared fine, and no one could tell I was struggling mightily with an unknown force continually pressing upon me to take my own life.

Through prayer, fasting, and worship, I asked God to change our situation and deliver me from the suicidal thoughts that were trying to overcome me. And He intervened by causing the suicidal thoughts to subside. But all else remained. I was still caught up with dealing with strange occurrences that challenged my sanity and faith in God.

But God's Word gave me some comfort and encouraged me to continue on. In the book of Second Corinthians we read about Paul seeking God's intervention in a painful and bothersome circumstance in his life. He asked three times for God to remove what Paul only described as a thorn in his flesh. But God told him, *"My grace is sufficient for you, for my power is made perfect in weakness"* (2 Corinthians 12:9a).

So I remained resolute knowing that God's ways and thoughts are higher than mine, and that His plans for my daughter and me remained good.

After arriving back home in Georgia, I continued to put on a façade to the outside world that all was well with us. However, of course, the reality was far different. I knew I needed to seek help. And one morning after leaving a meeting with my attorney, who had helped establish my non-profit organization, *Grace for Mile 6*, I felt prompted to call my friend—my sister-friend, who went with me and Camilla to visit that megachurch out of state.

I knew my friend attended a church whose worship was similar to that of Pentecostal worship. After she answered her phone, my very first question to her was, "Do you trust your pastor?"

Her response to me was, "I trust him fully."

She then shared with me her pastor's phone number.

I called him immediately while still in the parking lot of the lawyer's office. I introduced myself and shared what had been happening to my daughter and me. The pastor invited us to his church, and we attended the church's service the following Sunday. At our first visit, I realized that the worship style was similar to that of an Apostolic church we had attended when we first moved to Georgia. And I felt okay being there.

I had the opportunity after the service to talk with the pastor one-on-one. Following our conversation, the pastor decided to schedule one of his associate pastors to come pray with us and bless our home. I was glad for such a kind gesture, which showed he was truly concerned.

Prior to his visit to our home, the associate pastor asked that I buy a bottle of grape juice. And I did. I thought he was thirsty and needed something to drink. Oh, how naïve I was! The juice, it turned out, was to be used for a completely different reason. I failed to make the connection between the grape juice and that which it represented—the blood of Jesus as it relates to Communion.

But further, I had no way of knowing that God would use the series of events that started with the pastor's visit to eventually teach me more of the knowledge I needed to deal with our experiences. And I couldn't have imagined how God would in time teach me more about how Communion provides to us a glimpse into the true magnitude of the power of our Savior's blood.

I was already seeking help from God, and that led to me making a new appeal for help from my sister-friend's pastor. But I never could have dreamed how the connections I was beginning to make would be used by God to lead me toward having my life transformed by the power of the Holy Spirit.

However, before that could happen, the Holy Spirit first had to reveal to me certain connections between my experiences and my family's secrets.

CHAPTER 5

The Family's Secrets

For there is nothing hidden that will not become evident, nor anything secret that will not be known and come out into the open. (Luke 8:17 AMP)

IT WAS PERHAPS our second time to attend my friend's church. And each time we attended, it seemed I learned a bit more about different types of worship and praise that, frankly, ran contrary to what I knew from our Catholic worship. Everyone came prepared to dance to some of the most beautiful African worship songs I never knew existed.

My mother, though, knew some of the songs. They seemed to be in line with what she had learned from home. She danced her heart out with other members of the congregation, while my daughter and I merely swayed from side-to-side as we were all captivated by the level of devotion displayed by the members.

Some of the people kicked off their shoes. Others danced around the entire perimeter of the auditorium, while still others shook whatever instrument he or she had brought to church. It was amazing to watch. No, we were not spectators in the house of God; we were participants with an appreciation of something new in our lives.

But through it all, in the back of my mind I was wondering if the associate pastor would soon pay us his visit at our home. (He had not yet come to visit us.) I was eagerly anticipating him coming to visit and pray for us because I believed his help was the most effective way to counter what we faced.

But I had to push those thoughts aside as I became distracted. Looking up while there in church, I suddenly saw what looked to be several S-shaped figures flying in the air directly in front of me.

The music was loud, and it seemed to be disturbing whatever those things were. I remembered seeing the same things around me before, and I had even felt them on my body—"But now! In the house of God?" I asked. "Are they traveling with me?"

I became perplexed.

After the service, I made my way in line to talk with the pastor again about what I had seen.

My friend who recommended the church to me told me the church conducted deliverance services. Mind you, that was all new to me, so I knew very little of what all that entailed. All I knew was that we needed help.

I was told those deliverance meetings were hosted by several other pastors, and they would also *prophesy* during their attempts to cast out whatever evil spirit there was in the person. I found out that church was actually one of many branches of a megachurch with its main headquarters outside of the United States.

Again, without asking more questions, and without stopping to do any research, I took a friend's word at face value and dived in. But to my defense, I was desperate for help for my daughter and me, and I didn't know any better. After all, I *was* seeking help from a *church*!

I soon made my way into the pastor's office with my daughter and mother. And there, since I was told he was familiar with spiritual attacks, I asked him several questions hoping for answers from a spiritual point of view. As I understood it at the time, a spiritual attack is an affliction from the enemy. And I realized I needed help dealing with that enemy.

As I talked with the pastor, I noticed he hesitated to answer most of my questions. Instead, his eyes seemed fixed on my mother. I also believe he was uncomfortable discussing whatever it was that he had come to know about my family and me in front of my daughter.

He was very vague when answering my questions. So although I knew there was more to things than what he said, I did not press the matter. I simply acknowledged whatever little insight he gave and ended the conversation.

Following that, I enlisted my mother and daughter to begin attending the church's Wednesday night services with me and participating in what they call "Fire Night," which is a night service that begins at 9:00 PM and often lasts until 3:00 or 4:00 AM the next morning.

The Lord spoke through Jeremiah to the children of Israel in captivity in Babylon and said, *"You will seek me and find me when you seek me with all your heart"* (Jeremiah 29:13).

I was desperately searching for answers from Christ and His Bride—the Church.

I then assumed a hectic spiritual schedule as I began attending services at both the Catholic church and at that non-denominational church. But it was as if a level of supernatural strength had been given to me. I endured driving the long commutes to the non-denominational church that was about forty-five minutes one way from my home. And between three to four times a week, I also made the forty-five minute drive to attend evening services and the 9:00 AM Mass at the Catholic church.

I have to assume that since God knew what was ahead of me, the Holy Spirit had prompted me to make worship a priority. And previously, the extent of that worship was at a level contrary to anything I knew. But I was being drawn into the presence of God through fasting, prayer, and worship—through both singing and other acts of adoration—as best I knew how.

Ironically, I never felt weighed down with that kind of schedule. I instead often felt restless if I were to run late or miss any church services whether at the Catholic church or the new church. Also, when not in church I constantly listened to worship music and invested myself in praising God.

In spite of what had become a thorn in my flesh and an avalanche around me, I feel my obedience to that level of devotion overshadowed the ill intent of the enemy and kept me afloat.

But I somehow knew more was required of me. So although I was already volunteering at the Catholic church on Sunday evenings, I began volunteering at the new church when there was a need. My goal was to be active in the things of God as much as I could. And it seemed like my service to the church was the only thing that I was still able to do well. It was as if something new was beginning to take place in me and everything old was beginning to shut down.

The enemy had come to steal, kill, and destroy. But I had become like David, when he said, *"I was glad when they said to me, 'Let us go to the house of the LORD'"* (Psalm 122:1 NLT).

The associate pastor was finally scheduled to visit us, and I wondered how he would receive my story. "What will he think of me? After all, when I first sought help from a church, a ministry leader warned me not to *dabble in two worlds.* Will he do the same thing?"

My thoughts raced, and I attempted to put my mind at ease until his arrival, but I kept looking at the clock waiting for him to arrive. He finally arrived much later than his scheduled arrival time, but he did come. I showed him I appreciated his time and welcomed him.

While I already let you know I had some level of apprehension over his visit, I have to say I had played out many more details in my mind about how the visit would go, and it definitely turned out far differently than I imagined. But that will become clear to you as I continue my story.

I had the grape juice he requested on my kitchen counter and a bottle of olive oil to use for anointing, which I didn't have to buy because I was already loaded up with bottles of olive oil. My daughter and I had been using the oil to anoint ourselves in the morning and before going to bed.

After the pastor entered our living room, he placed his Bible on the coffee table and then began pacing back and forth across the floor while praying in tongues. I stood toward the middle of the room between the pastor and my mother, who sat in what had become her favorite chair. And it was evident that she was unmoved by the pastor's presence.

Then the pastor stopped pacing, looked at my mother, and said, "Mommy, stand up." (It's customary for Africans to refer to an elderly person with such a title due to the difference in age.)

My mother stood up, and he continued, "Mommy, are you ready to save your children?"

My mother's response was nonchalant. She became defensive at the pastor's question. The pastor, however, was undeterred. He pressed her further. He said, "Mommy, I am hearing, pointing to his ear, that no one will die.[5] You need to acknowledge the truth and save your children."

I mean, that interaction was playing out as if I were watching a movie. As the pastor continued to press her, my mother became angry and agitated. And at that point I seemed to be the only person who hadn't a clue of what the conversation was about.

The pastor then furiously looked at me and said, "Your mother knows what has been happening to you."

At that, my mother became angrier and began to display her usual antics when cornered with something unpleasant. My focus then turned back to the pastor. "What do you mean?" I asked.

He did not answer me but walked toward the kitchen and grabbed the anointing oil. He then anointed my home with both the oil and the grape juice (using the grape juice as the symbol of the blood of Christ).

My mother was quickly back in her chair showing no cause for concern and displaying a lack of emotion that I could not

5 My mother did not want to share the truth because she feared the enemy's retaliation against her family.

fathom. After the pastor finished blessing the home, he took me by the hand, and we walked into another room away from my mother.

As we both sat down, I could sense his frustration as he related to me the following:

"There's an altar against you."

"An altar? What is an altar?" I inquired

He said, "It's ancestral. It is something that has been in your family for generations. You are being nominated to take possession of it now. And you have to build your altar to counter the one that is fighting against you."

I asked, "How is this done?"

He then shared with me that there are a variety of ways an altar is established through the means of "true spiritual exercise."

We then ended our conversation. He politely said his goodbyes to us and left. After he left I immediately walked into the living room and endeavored to find out more about what the pastor shared.

As you may imagine, I was just as unsuccessful getting any information from my mother as the pastor had been. She did not change her position. Instead, she assured me that she would never do anything to hurt us—meaning all of her children.

By then it was late into the night, so we got ready for bed. We followed our usual routine by worshiping and praying before we all lay down to sleep. But going to sleep was not going to be easy for me.

While lying awake in bed processing what had happened that night, my mind began to go back to my childhood as I started to remember what I saw and experienced.

As a child, I was always sick. I was so ill that my family concluded I had sickle cell disease. I remembered that I was often sickly up until I left to live with my father in Italy as a young teenager, but I always bounced back from those episodes. Then I began to recall visits from distant families. I remembered being told as a child that they came to my late grandmother for "healing."

Both the visitors and my grandmother spoke Swahili since they were all from Congo, so we never understood what was said between them. But I remembered us children being told in a vague fashion that Mamma could help people who were suffering, and that was a gift she'd had since childhood.

That information was all we knew. For the most part, my siblings and I were never allowed to stick around when Mamma was helping them. The truth is, we were clueless most of the time when it came to what the adults were doing.

I remember lying there thinking how odd it was that those memories were coming to me that night when none of them had come to mind over all the preceding years. It's clear to me now that God was unearthing things from my past to present to me a picture of my family that I never knew existed.

Suddenly, a significant memory burst into my consciousness. Only God could have caused me to remember it. It was a memory of something that happened to me and my late brother, Richmond, when we were very young.

We were still living in the home where we were both born. And it was in the middle of the night when my late grandma and her husband, our step-grandfather, woke us up from our sleep. They brought Richmond and me into the living room. The lights were out, so my grandma held a lamp in her hand as they prepared for what had suddenly and remarkably become so vivid in my mind.

What they did next began with Richmond. My step-grandpa took Richmond by the hand and placed two cuts with a razor blade on each of his outer wrists. Then he applied what looked like ashes on the cuts. Then it was my turn. He did the same to me and placed ashes on the cuts on both of my outer wrists too.

I don't remember if we cried or what else occurred, but that event from the past came alive in me that night as I lay in bed. And I began to question if that experience began some kind of initiation for us while we were yet children.

I then wondered about the connection between that and my current experiences.

I know the Holy Spirit was at work revealing to me something I needed to know. "Was that our initiation into the practice of idol worship?" I pondered. "What was the significance of that ritual, and why had no one ever spoken to us about that throughout our lives?"

What do you do in a moment like that? I couldn't cry. And I couldn't press my mother any further about it, because I knew what her response would be like. So with that in mind, I decided to just rest in the Lord, who had begun a special work by revealing to me hidden family secrets.

Like the psalmist, I settled into continuing to place my hope in God and trust Him because of His faithfulness to me during my lifetime. *"O LORD, you alone are my hope. I've trusted you, O LORD, from childhood"* (Psalm 71:5 NLT).

Then ready to put all of it to rest for the night, I turned on the worship music that my daughter and I had started playing throughout the night. I tried to fall asleep but was unable to do it. And just as unexpected as events of the day had already been, so was what happened next.

While lying there trying to go to sleep I began to feel something crawling above my lips toward my nose, and the sensation was from within contrary to how it previously was with my head. It surprised and puzzled me. I rubbed my upper lip and tried to stop it. Then the feeling moved behind my left ear.

"What now?" I sighed. I then prayed quietly until I was able to fall asleep.

I kept all of that from my mother and daughter. I determined then that it was just between me and God. We continued our normal routine, but as we did, I continued seeking to learn more about our family's secrets.

CHAPTER 6

The Deliverance Process

Deliver me from my enemies, O God; be my fortress against those who are attacking me. (Psalm 59:1)

I CONTACTED THE lead pastor at the new church and followed up to discuss with him what his associate pastor had shared with me. He agreed that my mother had certain insight into things. Then he suggested that we begin what he called a "deliverance process," which would involve several pastors from the same ministry. I believed I was being led on the right path, so I agreed with him.

Our first prayer meeting that was part of the *deliverance process* was held locally at a prayer camp not far from our home. At the campsite, the lead pastor organized prayer and fasting retreats for members facing what they called "spiritual battles." My mother, daughter, and I arrived late in the afternoon to meet with the pastor, who was already praying in church at the campsite.

We joined in with the prayers, and shortly thereafter he began what he said was a "deliverance." My mother was the first to be addressed by the pastor. I was curious to see what the process entailed.

As I watched, the pastor began to pray over my mother, with whom he was now face-to-face with their hands tightly gripped in a locked position. As he prayed, he occasionally loosened his grip with one hand, tapped with his fingers on her forehead, and with a stern voice commanded something to leave by saying, "Come out of her!"

I continued watching as then the pastor and my mother began to spin in a circular motion. They eventually spun at a speed that made it seem they were ready to take off until my mother ended up lowering herself down on the floor. By that, according to the pastor, She had been "delivered"

My mother got up and sat down where she had been. The pastor then took my daughter by the hand and began her *deliverance*. She went through the same process as my mother, only she didn't spin around as many times as my mother, and her *deliverance* was brief. She then sat next to her grandmother.

When it became my turn, I held the pastor's hands as he began to pray over me. I, too, got a few taps on the forehead with the same command as that spoken over my mother. "Come out of her!" Then I too began to spin violently in a circular motion with the pastor holding me tightly. It felt like forever, but it was brief. Then I was lowered to the floor like the others. It was like the wind knocked me out. I was exhausted.

After regaining my composure, the pastor, who was then standing by one of the windows staring outside as he continued to pray in tongues, asked me, "What is the meaning of *Laura?*"

I answered, "I don't know." And I continued to say that my mother told me she named me Laura after her favorite late cousin, and that she had yielded to everyone's demands that I would be named Laura after my birth.

The pastor's response to that was one neither my mother nor I anticipated. He asked, "Who's Elizabeth?"

Again I answered and said, "It's my middle name."

He then said, "Elizabeth is the name the Lord recognizes for you. I hear the Lord say Elizabeth is the river."

After hearing that, I lifted both of my hands in the air and said, "Lord, let me flow wherever you want me to flow."

All that while, my mother sat quietly and never participated in the discussion between me and the pastor.

I wanted to know what the spinning was all about, so I asked him. The pastor shared that those were what he called "manifestations." He continued, "It's the Power of God that is doing a work in you."

Well, what further explanation would anyone need after hearing that the power of God is at work in you? So after that, we said our goodbyes and left.

We planned on spending the weekend at my sister-friend's house, and in the car while driving to her place, I thanked my mother for participating in the *deliverance.* I promised to honor and take care of her until God called her home. I vowed that she would never lack, because she had sacrificed in letting go of what had been in the family.

She actually showed a bit of excitement and then responded by saying, "I'm innocent and will do anything for my children."

A sense of relief came over me.

When we arrived at my sister-friend's place, I called her outside and shared with her what had happened in the prayer garden (which is what they call it). That was actually the first time I had ever talked with her about what had been going on with my daughter and me. We both hugged each other and thanked God.

I was thrilled. But as we made our way back toward her apartment, I suddenly saw what looked like a full human being in the form of a black shadowy figure in front of me. I didn't say anything since the encounter was brief, but I felt a sinking feeling. We proceeded into her apartment, where we stayed as planned.

I felt compelled to give a testimony of our "deliverance" at church the following Sunday. I was very much excited to share, so when it was testimony time, I went up front and shared about what the pastor had done at the prayer garden and what my experience had been over the weekend. I hadn't felt the crawling, nor had I seen the S-shaped figures dancing around me since then.

I talked about how my life had changed since everything started in December of 2018, and I concluded by saying I was eager to embark on a new chapter in my life.

But Mio Dio! (That means, "My God!" in Italian.) My assertion was an illusion!

I was soon thrust even further into mysteries. And only the Almighty God, whose power supersedes all others, kept us from being consumed by my opponents. I pluralize the word *opponent* because I found out later that many evil attacks were planned against me with the intention of either killing me or having me lose my mind and become a beggar on the streets.

Thank God for His promises.

And such as do wickedly against the covenant shall he corrupt by flatteries: but the people that do know their God shall be strong, and do exploits.   (Daniel 11:32 KJV)

I knew with whom my daughter and I had a covenant. We had a covenant with God. And the assurances of the promises of the Most High God, whose Word is as sure as the breath I breathe, laid the map for the rest of the roads I would travel.

Earlier in the day I rejoiced about being delivered. But that night I had a dream about a friend's daughter who had just died. In the dream she brought some food to my house and was very happy to see me. She hugged me as she placed the food in my refrigerator. My mother was also with us in the dream, and she stood and watched.

Then, in the morning when I woke up after having the dream, I again began to see a full silhouette of a black shadow, and it soon became an object that was following me and dancing around me. I decided to not hesitate but take quick action to deal with that. And I decided to not rely on my mother. Instead, I called home to Freetown to ask questions of other members of the family.

I placed a call to one of my brothers and asked him if they had seen or experienced what I was seeing and experiencing. He said, "Yes." Then I asked to speak to my younger nieces and youngest brother, whom I asked the same question, and their responses were also, "Yes."

So what some of them experienced had then been introduced to my daughter and me. After speaking with my family back home in Freetown, it was time to again question my mother. I asked her if she had experienced the same thing I had just experienced, and I made sure she knew I had talked with my siblings and nieces back home.

Faced with that, my mother admitted that she, too, had experienced the same thing back at home and also while with me in my home.

I then asked her if my late grandma had also experienced it, and she said, "Yes." She further told me that the shadowy presence had caused my late grandmother to go blind, and she needed an operation to restore her eyesight.

I then inquired as to why she hadn't shared any of that with me. Again, I wanted to know what it all had to do with me—and also with my daughter, since she also was by then seeing the same shadowy figure or image all around us.

I got the usual answer from my mother, "I don't know." Which of course didn't help anything.

I then called the lead pastor who had done the *deliverance* and shared that added mystery with him. He advised me to see another pastor who was also a part of their team but whose "anointing" matched our "spiritual warfare." The pastor followed that by setting up a meeting for us. And when the time came, I went to the meeting with my mother and daughter.

I started to notice that each time we left for a meeting such as those, my mother always wore African attire that she brought from home. My mother had a closet full of clothes I had purchased for her while in America. Nonetheless, that African outfit was what she wore each time. I became concerned about it, but I let the matter be. I had bigger fish to fry.

Before we left to see that pastor, I made sure we prayed and followed our devotional routine. I even fasted. And I continued to pray quietly all throughout the commute while listening to my favorite gospel radio station. When we arrived, I sensed that the pastor was far more outspoken than his peers.

He was bubbly and smiled often. He was not an introvert like the other two. He made us feel comfortable. But in contrast, my mother's countenance was the same as usual—unmoved, unfriendly, and angry. I didn't let it bother me, though. I needed answers and wanted God to direct us through the vessels He had chosen for their specialized tasks.

As Paul wrote in Ephesians:

> And he gave some, apostles; and some, prophets; and some, evangelists; and some, pastors and teachers; For the perfecting of the saints, for the work of the ministry, for the edifying of the body of Christ.   (Ephesians 4:11-12 KJV)

I didn't know what my entire family had pledged to *whomever.* I didn't know to whom or what we children had been promised and in what capacity. I just knew I was determined to stay within the confines of God's constraints. So I felt it was my responsibility to trust the pastors over my mother, who was unwilling to talk.

The pastor wanted to meet with me privately, so he called me into his office and sat me down directly across from him. Looking at me sternly, he asked, "Do you know who you are?"

My mind began to race. "What?" I thought to myself. My eyes must have been as wide as a football field. "What type of question is this?"

I don't even remember answering before I heard him say, "When you come into your own, all you will do is speak, and it will come to pass."

"OK, what's happening here?" I thought.

He continued, "You are gifted. They are fighting you because of your gift."

"They, who're they?" Thoughts bounced around in my head like they wouldn't stop.

At that point, I couldn't say a word; I was speechless. Then, I heard, "Call your mother."

I opened the door and beckoned my mother into the pastor's office. She sat down next to me. Then he said to her, "Have you told your daughter the truth? Your daughter must know the truth."

"Alright," I thought, "this is now the third pastor who has confronted my mother about a hidden truth or secret!"

What came from my mother was one of her typical, belligerent answers. "I don't have anything to say."

I mentioned the pastor was outspoken, right? He countered my mother's response with this:

"You are lying."

Then he dropped one of the most powerful bombs thus far. "When your daughter was little, she was sick almost always. And she almost died. You took her from one alternative native doctor to another seeking her healing. You promised those native doctors that if they would heal your daughter, she would be theirs."

My mother then became visibly upset, and left with no alternative, she said, "Yes, but I only took her to one place."

To that, the pastor said, "Untrue."

He then turned his attention to me and said, "Your intelligence level at the age of three was that of an eight-year-old. You are brilliant and gifted."

At that, I shared with him that my mother told me I was the only one of all of her children who walked at the age of seven months. But I told him that was all I knew of my childhood. I knew nothing about gifts and intellects.

He then said, "They've done a lot to you."

"A lot? Such as . . . ?" I wondered.

"They have taken your hair, nails, et cetera, to do evil with it."

That blew my mind, and I clearly did not expect to hear what came next.

"All those snakes in your body will die one by one."

"Whoa! What now?" My mind raced. "How can I answer such a thing when I haven't got a clue about what all this means? The crawling on my head and body is the result of an ill spiritual attack projected into my body?"

It was foreign to me, but for once, something was beginning to make sense about the crawling sensations and the S-shaped figures.

The pastor ended by saying that we needed to fast for several days. He said he would organize the fast and prayer time and get back to us.

The drive home was simply eerie. My mother was furious with me. My mind was preoccupied, and I didn't know how to take it all in. But thankfully, Camilla was not privy to what was shared since she was not in the pastor's office with my mother and me. The atmosphere was the same when we arrived home. Things seemed to be spiraling out of control so fast that I felt I was sinking and needed a lifejacket.

My mother gave me the cold shoulder for the rest of the evening. I continued our usual routine without allowing a break from what was holding us together—prayer and worship. Once in bed, I began processing what I had learned and tried to make sense of what was said. Nothing made sense, though. I could not even begin to apply all the things the pastor said and understand how my mother could continue to be so defiant.

A shift occurred for me at that point. I needed to get deeper into the mysteries. I called my brother in Freetown again. I told him what the pastor said. That opened up another conversation between my brother and me. In it, my brother told me my late uncle, (the one whose funeral I attended in Africa) had shared "deep family secrets" with him before his death.

My brother talked about mysteries that supposedly none of the children knew, but that the rest of the adults did. I attended that uncle's funeral, and I was involved in many family meetings while I was there in Africa. I stayed in a house with that brother and another sibling along with my nieces and nephew. I wondered why that was not discussed with me then.

My brother touched on a few things that my late uncle had done but those didn't pertain to the family or me. Rather, they were simply things that one would deem selfish and hateful toward others. But then he said my late uncle told him our great-grandparents and others in the family had done the unthinkable as it relates to worshiping idols.

"What more is my family hiding?" I wondered. "Could the pastor have been right when he said my family is responsible for what is happening to my daughter and me?"

I then remembered my family's pastor back in Freetown and decided to call him. I met him only once—while in Africa for my uncle's funeral—but I thought he could tell me something to shed light on my family's background and actions in the past.

While I was in Africa that time, family members invited me to attend their church with them. I had never met their pastor before, but during the service he called for first-time visitors to stand so he could pray for us. I stood up. It was while he was praying that he came toward me and said, "I see the spirit of death all over you."

Of course, being a believer, I prayed against what he said and trusted in God to protect me—not realizing there could be much more at stake than what was said.

So following the conversation with my brother, I called to see what that pastor knew about my family, if anything. The pastor, who it turns out had been privy to some information, proceeded to tell me certain things that seemed to confirm what my brother had shared with me.

It was during that conversation when the pastor also said, "Your mother should not have joined you in the U.S.."

Man, it was deep!

I am electing to write mostly about my experiences and not about what my brother and their family pastor shared. Ultimately, I hope my experiences will point you to God and not to the opposition. And my attempt to do that is intentional. I refuse to celebrate or purposely give a platform to the works of the enemy. God deserves center stage, and putting Him in that position is the intended purpose of this book.

I could write more, but suffice it to say right now that regardless of what the pastors I had been dealing with might have thought, their *deliverance process* had not met my needs.

CHAPTER 7

Saying Goodbye

Thus says the LORD God: "It shall not stand, nor shall it come to pass." (Isaiah 7:7 NKJV)

LIFE AT HOME was just getting tougher. I didn't say a word to my mother about having spoken to my brother and their pastor. And while continuing our routine, I became vigilant at observing everything my mother did. I also began to experience a drastic physical change in my body that I hadn't experienced before. I felt like I was on fire—blazing with discomfort.

I went from experiencing crawling sensations on my head, ear, and face to my entire body. I remember waking up one morning and starting to go about my usual custom. I took a cup of coffee in my hand, and as I took a sip, it was like someone had lit a can of gasoline on fire in my stomach. It was like an explosion in my belly.

I let out a scream that startled both my mother and daughter. My daughter was concerned and came toward me to see if I was

OK. My mother, though, remained seated in her favorite chair, unmoved, and never bothered to check on me. From then on, I also began to feel like something was crawling in my stomach.

That experience was a daily occurrence. And there were times I was so nauseous that I got the feeling of throwing up, but I couldn't. My mouth salivated so often that, when driving, I had to make frequent stops on the roads to spit. I was miserable because something I was dealing with was seemingly overtaking my entire body.

But I knew I was not alone. Before the Children of Israel entered the Promised Land—where they were to battle against the fierce occupants of the land—God promised to never leave or forsake them. And I knew God would not leave or forsake me as I battled against the enemies of my soul in what I by then realized was a battle against spiritual darkness.

And I believe it was only the Holy Spirit who empowered me to stand on Scripture and trust God at that time to go before me into the battle.

So be strong and courageous! Do not be afraid and do not panic before them. For the LORD your God will personally go ahead of you. He will neither fail you nor abandon you.

(Deuteronomy 31:6 NLT)

I knew I had to hold on to God's Word while I gathered up the courage to live with my mother, who I then knew was a suspect and contributor to me having to experience so many unpleasant things.

I soon began to observe a few other changes. For instance, from the time she came to live with us, my mother had been sleeping in the same room with me. And beginning only after learning more about my family's secrets, the Holy Spirit started waking me up in the middle of the night every time my mother got up to use the restroom. And those wake-up calls weren't soft taps; they were forceful jerkings that caused me to jump.

One night when I woke up, I saw her toss one of the throw pillows underneath the bed as she got up. I was fully awake and saw it clearly. That was a strange thing for her to do, and for the life of me I couldn't imagine why she did it.

I actually called out to my mother to make sure she knew I was awake. Then, as she walked to the bathroom, I got up and looked underneath the bed to see why she would have tossed the throw pillow under the bed. But when I looked under the bed, no pillow was there. There was absolutely nothing under the bed! I looked around, and it turned out the throw pillow wasn't even anywhere in the room.

But even more strange, alarming, and confusing—whatever you want to call it—as I continued searching for the pillow, I finally found it in another room where my daughter was sleeping.

Talk about having a moment!

I returned to bed and lay there dumbfounded as I wondered what it all could mean. But when my mother came back from the restroom, we both acted as if nothing had taken place.

Several strange things kept happening, and as they did, I kept my thoughts from my mother and only shared them with the pastors still working on our deliverance. The lead pastor was inclined to send us to several deliverance services to include one with a pastor in New Jersey.

But the more we attended those services, the stranger the episodes became. I continued to dream many dreams, and so did my mother, who shared her dreams with me. Interestingly, her dreams were of my family, particularly one of my brothers and his father—my mother's ex-husband. And it turned out that I, too, had dreamed similar dreams of them.

I then started believing my mother was seeking information from me by sharing her dreams. I decided she wanted to know what I knew. One morning after she woke up and shared with me another one of her dreams, an unusual level of boldness came upon me, and I respond firmly to her.

I said, "Please let your son and ex-husband know to stop whatever it is they are doing. Otherwise, you will bury them both as you've buried your brother."

Now, I knew that was straight from the Holy Spirit, because I would not have spoken like that on my own.

My mother turned and looked at me but was at a loss for words. And shortly after that exchange, her son I referred to called my mother to let her know his father had become paralyzed and was confined to a wheelchair. He never recovered and eventually died shortly after that.

I am not suggesting the exchanges between my mother and me resulted in her ex-husband's demise. I'm simply telling you what happened. But I was learning through all my experiences—both the good ones and the bad ones—that my and my daughter's lives were in the hands of God. And He was teaching me throughout all my ordeals that I had to trust and believe in His knowledge, wisdom, and sovereignty.

My relationship with my mother was no longer what it was when she came to live with us. The excitement had fizzled, and I no longer trusted her. She, too, became cold toward her granddaughter and me. At that point, I openly told her I would not participate in whatever she and other family members had participated in or serve whatever they pledged to serve.

I declared to her in no uncertain terms that my daughter and I only recognized one God, and it was to Him whom we belong.

Interestingly, the more I asserted my position to her, the more challenging the afflictions became for me. Physically, I felt if there were actually such a thing as the walking-dead, I was one of them. But to battle against my afflictions I began to press more into fasting, prayer, and worshiping.

God continued to show himself faithful to me as He allowed the Holy Spirit to direct me about being in tune with Him and not allowing the situation to consume me. Also, I assure you that my daughter was active in those spiritual exercises with me.

In addition to our spiritual exercises at home, the non-denominational church had us engage in a rigorous deliverance prayer and fasting schedule. One day, the pastor—the one who revealed what had occurred in my childhood—came to our house for prayer. Well, I can't say the meeting was much different from the one when we visited him at his church.

He continued to further expose my mother by sharing more family secrets that my mother could not refute but refused to acknowledge. And her response and countenance appeared to only confirm the pastor's position.

My mother stood directly in front of the pastor with an anger that could kill. She was furious. But he was not concerned about her feelings and remained resolute in revealing what the Holy Spirit had shown him.

When it was time for the pastor to leave, he prayed and blessed our home. But before he said his goodbyes, he cautioned my mother about the role she and others in my family played and continued to play in all that was happening to my daughter and me.

However, as far as my mother was concerned, it was as if he were talking to a brick wall. As for me, I could only resort to what I knew—God's Word. As the pastor prayed before leaving, I prayed with him resolutely and fervently, because I was becoming fearful over all I was hearing about the level of the family's deep secrets that had been hidden from me but were then being brought to light.

In the end, the pastor left without gaining any ground with my mother.

Soon after that pastor's visit, the lead pastor suggested that my mother, daughter, and I should be water baptized. I shared with him that we had been baptized with water when my mother came from Freetown. But the lead pastor urged us to be baptized again. Don't ask me why.

I adhered to his recommendation and prepared for all of us to be baptized again. When the time came, however, my mother refused to participate, but my daughter and I were again baptized.

After our baptism, we went to the mall to spend some time before going out to eat a few hours later. As we were leaving the mall to head to the car, a man called out to me. I had seen the man standing inside one of the department stores with a bag in his hand as if he had made a purchase.

There had been no verbal exchange between us as we walked past him going inside. Strangely, though, as we were walking out to leave the mall, the same man followed us out and asked if I was from an African country. I responded by letting him know what part of Africa I was from. He then walked off, and we proceeded to our car.

Now what I am going to share with you will blow your mind.

When we got onto the highway, the same man was driving alongside me and waving to us the entire drive until we exited. As we did, he was there beside us again on the access road waving and smiling to us. I didn't think a lot more about it (beside it being a bit strange) other than he was nice.

When we arrived at the restaurant, my daughter couldn't find one of her shoes. My daughter was convinced that she had on both of her shoes when she got in the car, and she took them off in the car—as she has in the habit of doing. We looked everywhere in my car and did not find the shoe. I even drove back to the mall and canvassed the parking lot with no success at finding her shoe.

That was such an odd experience, and to this day there is no explanation for what happened to the shoe. But I also noted that the man we saw bore a strange resemblance to my late uncle Kofi. I then said to my mother, who was in the car with us, "The man at the mall looked exactly like your brother, Uncle Kofi."

With a nervous grin, my mother said, "I thought so myself." She continued, "Even the way he smiled."

I sensed something terrible was at play. I felt my daughter had become the target of a spiritual attack. But I was encouraged by the Word of God.

Lo, children are an heritage from the LORD: and the fruit of the womb is his reward. (Psalm 127:3 KJV)

I knew my daughter was covered under the protection of God by the shed blood of Jesus Christ.

During the night following our baptism I had a strange dream of a man saying he was not pleased with our baptism. Of course I recognized what the dream was about. I kept the dream to myself and prayed a simple prayer as I lay in bed.

After waking up the next morning I read a text message another brother had sent to me during the night. He shared in the message that our cousin passed away during the night. That cousin was my late uncle Kofi's only son, who had been afflicted with madness several years earlier.

I wondered if his death could have been another intervention by the hand of God to protect us. I could not say for sure. But I knew that a spirit of madness was something that the enemy had sometimes projected into our family. On a couple of occasions my mother had also experienced temporary insanity but fully regained her mental functions. I considered that could be another way of the enemy to gain compliance to what they had pledged.

So many things were happening, and they were happening so fast that I was struggling to keep up with all of it. But I learned to keep my thoughts to myself and survive one day at a time—all the while suffering both physically and mentally. I dealt with continual discomfort in my body, and I was getting concerned about what felt like a rapid decline of my own mental ability.

I continued to press the lead pastor for answers. And then he and the team suggested that I send my mother back to Africa because she was what they called the *Point of Contact.*

I struggled to understand the necessity behind such drastic action. I mean, I labored to relocate her to America. I spent a lot of money on the process. Most importantly, though, I knew bringing her here could provide another opportunity for my family to improve, since with my support she could eventually bring more of her children to the U.S.—where they too could gain independence.

Many years of planning coupled with good intentions seemed futile. I prayed and sought answers from God about the pastor's counsel. But He seemed silent on giving me any direct answers. However, I eventually found that the answers I was seeking were to arrive through more of my experiences in the midst of my storm.

Life didn't get easier but grew worse.

Trusting in God's ability to transform both people and circumstances, I continued to take my mother to church with me and have her participate in every spiritual activity held by each church we attended. (We were still attending both Catholic Mass and services at the non-denominational church.)

My mother seemed invested in the church and in everything that was being done for us collectively as a family (except to share what she knew about the family's secrets). She danced her heart out during praise and worship. She participated in the Fire Night activities. She often fasted with me. She gave her tithe and offering along with me.

I watched as she did all of those things. I was hoping to see a difference in her and our circumstances. It became crystal clear to me, though, that my efforts were coming up short. But because of the promises of God, I refused to believe all was lost. Jesus said:

So I say to you: Ask and it will be given to you; seek and you will find; knock and the door will be opened to you. For everyone who asks receives; the one who seeks finds; and to the one who knocks, the door will be opened. (Luke 11:9-10)

I was seeking and knocking. I desired and prayed constantly for the salvation of my mother and family. But I also had to remind myself that the salvation and deliverance I prayed for could be realized only when those for whom I prayed desired the same thing with a sincere and repentant heart.

I was in the bathroom one evening getting ready for the night. Suddenly, I was prompted by the Holy Spirit to go outside, but I genuinely didn't know why. I left the bathroom and walked down the hall. As I did, I looked through the door of the bedroom where my mother kept her clothes. There, I saw my mother retrieving several papers from her purse.

She was startled when she saw me. Curious, I then walked into the other bedroom, where we slept, and pretended to be doing something. My mother soon joined me and sat on the bed. I deliberately focused my attention away from her while still watching her discreetly. I wanted to see what she was going to do with the papers in her hands.

My mother believed I was not looking, so she placed the documents under her pillow. I didn't know what the papers contained, but coupled with what I had been dreaming of my family, that behavior was yet another confirmation to me that my mother was hiding and doing something to me and my daughter—just as the pastors had told me. I walked out of the room and headed back to the bathroom without saying a word.

Like David, I knew I should not fret because of those who do evil (Psalm 37:1). So I resolved to trust that God was in control, but I took action.

I called my daughter to me and asked her to pack some things and grab her bag. I did the same. I told my mother we were leaving home for the night but would return in the morning. My mother is dark-skinned in completion, but the color of her face changed. She was startled. And I believe that was when she concluded she had been found out.

After that exchange, I walked off with Camilla and left my mother home alone. I wept bitterly as we drove off.

"How could this be?" I moaned inwardly. "My own family! My mother as the head! How is it possible for this person—who came to church with me, fasted with me, danced in the presence of God, and gave tithes and offerings to God—to mock God in this way? What could have such a hold on her that she's unmoved and unconcerned about the dangers of her actions? What pleasure could she gain by what she has been doing to cause her to defile our Lord and heap such calamity on her children?"

My thoughts were all over the place. I could not control myself. My daughter was in the back seat absorbing it all. After making the nearly one-hour drive to my friend's house, I had to regain my composure. I wondered how I could share with my sister-friend and her family my new reality. We knocked on her door, and when she opened the door, all I could say was, "We need to stay here for tonight."

She looked behind me for my mother, and when she didn't see her, she asked, "Where is your mother?" I didn't know how to answer her question with the truth. So I just said, "I left her home."

I lay on my friend's couch most of that night, unable to sleep. She's my mother after all, so I was troubled that I had left her alone. I felt sorry for her. I attempted to rationalize how I could make the situation better. I wanted to fix what was broken. And I wanted to pursue and destroy what had become the destroyer of my family.

I realize clearly now that the enemy uses people to do his dirty work. It would have helped me during that season if I had understood it at the time, but I didn't. Sometimes I wondered if my mother and siblings were perhaps just victims of circumstance. But I contrasted that against the actions of my mother that seemed not only voluntary but also almost enjoyable to her and without remorse.

I was overcome with emotions without remedy. But while deeply longing for something better, I fell asleep.

We woke up early in the morning since I needed to drop off my daughter at school. And while driving back to our place, I began to reflect on how I could face my mother. I could no longer rely on my strength while dealing with either her or with whatever she and the family had aligned themselves. I desperately needed my Heavenly Father's help.

I asked God for evidence that He was with me and would help me through the journey. Like Moses, I said, *"Now show me your glory"* (Exodus 33:18b). I wanted to hear God say to me like He said to Moses, *"I will cause all my goodness to pass in front of you"* (Exodus 33:19a).

I longed for the Lord to support me and guide me in the plight my daughter and I faced. And burdened down by the weight of our reality, it became a matter of life and death to me.

But even with that, I looked for ways to convince the pastors why my mother should stay in the United States.

I was still debating the matter in my mind as we arrived at my daughter's school. After letting my daughter out of the car I called the lead pastor to share what I had observed in my mother's possession. He was alarmed, and he asked that I go home to get the papers and bring them to the church, where he would be waiting for me.

I was both nervous and afraid at the same time. I somehow mustered the nerve and headed home. I met my mother, who as always it seemed was sitting in her favorite chair. I asked about her night and if she had eaten. She responded, "Yes."

I needed to distract her with something while I headed upstairs to search through her purse. So I offered to play one of her favorite movies, which is a Nigerian film. She said, "Yes," when I asked her if she wanted me to do that, so I did.

I puttered around downstairs with her for a bit before sneaking upstairs. I was a nervous wreck and sweating profusely as I opened my mother's closet. I hastily reached for her purse and pulled out a brown medium-sized envelope. I looked inside, which was a terrible mistake on my part.

Both of my hands began to shake, and I began to hyperventilate because of what I saw. I folded the envelope and put my mother's purse back into the closet. I raced downstairs and told my mother I needed to run a quick errand. I then drove out of my garage and parked a few feet away from the house. I had to cry for a while.

In the brown envelope that had my name written all over it, there were several birth certificates issued with my name. Each one contained my first and last name, but there was one with a middle name I never knew I had—Edith.

Both of the birth certificates contained discrepancies in my birth year, with one showing February 2, 1976, and the other February 2, 1977. But one certificate was certified in 2003 and the other in 2004. The birth certificates were not the only documents in the envelope containing information about me. Rather, every piece of paper in the envelope was about me. There were several very long sheets of papers with many of what looked like complex mathematics or Arabic writings all over them that seemed to me to give directions or instructions about me.

I looked again and found a SIM card for one of Freetown's phone companies wrapped in what looked like a thread. I then realized the handwriting on most of the papers was that of my late uncle, whose funeral I had attended the previous year.

I didn't need either the pastor or the Holy Spirit to confirm what the papers and SIM card represented. Undoubtedly, they were fetish items, and they confirmed that my family had been and were still involved in devilish practices. But not only that, they also proved that whatever had been pledged somehow involved me.

I finally regained my composure, placed the envelope on the passenger seat, and began the forty-five minute drive to the church. As I drove I continued to process everything and tried to come up with a reason for my mother bringing those documents with her from Freetown.

"What was she doing with them at night or when I was not at home?" I wondered. "How has this affected my daughter and me?"

Then I began to put the pieces of the puzzle together. There were the breathing issues, the crawling sensations, the many odd dreams, and the S-shaped figures dancing around and following my daughter and me everywhere we went.

Then there was the way I had been feeling so ill and weak at home after eating food, and I realized that often my mother would not eat that same food. Instead, she said she was not hungry even though she hadn't eaten. I often found that behavior strange, but who would suspect a mother of having ill-intent toward her own child and grandchild? I most certainly did not.

And as fast as those thoughts were going through my mind, another memory flashed into it. I remembered being away from home one day when I received a telephone call from another of my brothers. We talked cordially for quite a while, but something seemed amiss about the conversation. I thought his actions were strange, but I didn't give it a lot of thought.

When I returned home, I glanced at myself in the mirror as I made my way to my bedroom. And when I did, I realized that my left ear was covered with what looked like brown snakeskin. (I almost always talk on the phone with it on my left ear.)

I examined my ear and wondered if it had been there before that day without noticing it. But I thought I surely would have noticed it since it was so visible and odd looking. I then simply peeled off the scale and never thought about it again until that day I was driving to the church.

I know you may think I'm crazy, but I assure you it happened, and it was a physical covering on my ear that I was able to remove. I too thought it was weird, but back then, I didn't think about it having any connection to some kind of operation of the enemy.

As I approached the church with the envelope I honestly wasn't sure I wanted to see anyone at that point, so when the pastor sent to me a text message telling me he was running late and suggesting that I drop the package into the church's secure mailbox, I did so and left.

Later, the pastor informed me that all the things in the envelope were means by which my mother communicated with whatever "force" it was that had controlled the family for generations. He continued to say, "You are like Moses. Through you, your family will be set free. Your siblings are essentially non-existent, but through your prayers and diligence in seeking God, they are alive."

I was baffled by most of his words, but I knew the part about my siblings being non-existent was somewhat true. Troubled by all of that, I definitely needed to read what the Lord told the people through Isaiah.

Listen to me, you who pursue righteousness and who seek the LORD: *Look to the rock from which you were cut and to the quarry from which you were hewn.* (Isaiah 51:1)

Where else could I look? Who had what I needed—and what my family needed—except God?

After dropping off the envelope and its contents I returned home expecting my mother to confront me about her documents, but it never happened. I never retrieved the envelope or its contents from the pastor, and I waited for the next several days for my mother to say something about it—but nothing.[6] I didn't say anything, either. Instead, we just lived together contentiously.

We were living together but worlds apart. My daughter and I eventually started staying at home during the day but at my sister-friend's place each night. I was no longer comfortable sleeping in the same house with my mother.

The Bible says *"wisdom is profitable to direct."*[7] And I was trying my best to use wisdom in making my decisions. But the things that had transpired thus far appeared not to have convicted or moved my mother by any means. To the contrary, I became her enemy.

---

6   The pastor eventually gave the envelope with its contents to the pastor who revealed information about my childhood to see and burn.

7   "If the iron be blunt, and he do not whet the edge, then must he put to more strength: but wisdom is profitable to direct," (Ecclesiastes 10:10 KJV).

And that was an attitude she extended to her granddaughter as well.

It was evident that we were at the mercies of God. It was definitely a matter of life and death, and my mother was the *point of contact* for whatever desired to destroy my daughter and me or afflict me with insanity. For me, though, I somehow needed to continue being my mother's daughter, and that of God's, so I did my best to navigate the territory with wisdom.

In doing that, I continued to bring my mother to church with us. And I made sure she continued to receive her bi-weekly allocation of money that I arranged for her. But while doing that, I began secretly preparing to send her back to Freetown.

While I was at first resistant to the pastors' advice, it had become dangerous for me to have my mother at home with us. And the following episodes will illustrate that.

One Sunday morning after spending the night at my sister-friend's place, I was on the freeway getting ready to exit as I was driving home to pick up my mother to attend church. The roads were clear, and the few cars on the road were at a good distance from one another. As I approached our exit, a giant tire flew out of nowhere and struck my vehicle.

But the tire didn't come from the road I was driving on. No, it flew from somewhere else and just appeared at some height in front of me. The passenger side of my car was damaged, but thankfully, neither my daughter nor I was hurt. I prayed and continued on home.

Upon arriving home, I was met with a heavy smell of gas that had taken over the entire house, including upstairs. I panicked as

I raced to look for my mother. My mother, though, was resting comfortably in her chair, unbothered. I then became angry (mainly because I had actually previously dreamed of the incident but never identified my mother as someone who could have been responsible for it).

I called out to my mother and asked if she was OK, to which she responded, "I'm fine."

I asked if she could not smell the gas that had engulfed the entire house. She said, "No."

I told my mother to leave and walk outside while I opened the doors and windows to let some air in. She got up from the chair with an angry gesture of resistance. As she made her way through the garage, I heard her speaking in her native Swahili tongue. I looked at the stove and found the source of the leaking gas.

One of the knobs had been turned to the medium level.

My mother never cooked because she was afraid of using a gas stove. So why was the knob in an on position? Both the flying tire and the leaking gas incidents happened in a matter of thirty minutes apart. I decided my mother was responsible for the gas in an attempt to take us out because the first attempt on the road had failed.

As disappointed as I was, I asked my mother to get in the car, and we still took her to church with us. Exodus 20:12 says, *"Honor your father and your mother, so that you may live long in the land the* Lord *your God is giving you."*

Shortly thereafter, I completed the arrangements for my mother's return to Freetown. I kept our prayer and worship routine and our weekly church schedule, including the Fire Night and Wednesday night services. During all of them my mother's countenance was that of one of a faithful servant of our Most

High God. From the outside looking in, it never would have crossed anyone's mind that my mother joined any members of her family in dabbling in the other side.

I was determined to be obedient to the command of Exodus 20:12. My mother, though, treated me as an enemy. She instigated fights at every opportunity. Clearly, my refusal to disobey God was received as an insult to their occult practices.

During one of the more tense moments, I stood face-to-face with my mother in the living room and confronted her. I had enough of her playing the victim—blaming me for choices she and others had made.

I forcefully pointed out to my mother that I never signed up to carry any of their burdens.

My mother had pushed me to the point of explosion that day. I had come downstairs to get something. (During the day I mostly stayed in another room upstairs that had by that time become my and my daughter's place of refuge.) She met me in the kitchen with one of her many defensive tactics. But I was of no mind to either engage her or show her any mercy.

My life and that of my daughter had been turned upside down. Our health had been compromised. Our home had been violated. And my finances had been afflicted. Therefore, I could not feel empathy for my mother that day. Full of rage, I did not allow her to finish what she was trying to convey to me before I lashed out against her.

"I am going to kill that devil!" I shouted while stomping both of my feet on the kitchen floor in anger.

My mother is not one to back off, so she too stomped her feet as she responded back. "I have a devil?" she said back to me angrily.

I responded, "Yes, you do! It's been in the family!" Then I went further by saying, "Look at your children's lives—all of my brothers—they are a mess!" I then told her neither I nor my daughter and nieces would ever participate in that evil. I then began to share the strange things I had noticed in our lives since her arrival.

After that confrontation, I knew I was at the mercies of God because I didn't know what my mother and that which had assumed control of our family would do. But at the same time, I was not ignorant of the enemy's schemes,[8] and I relied on the greatness of the One who lives in me.

I went back to my room and trusted in the words of Moses to the children of Israel: *"The LORD himself will fight for you. Just stay calm"* (Exodus 14:14 NLT).

During that time, a few of my friends called and talked with my mother to inquire about life in the U.S., and she basically acted as if everything was great. (But I actually did the same.) No one knew of the dynamics of our relationship at home except the pastors working with us and my sister-friend, with whom I shared a few things.

How do you begin to share with people that your family has been living a lie all their lives? It was best to keep my newfound reality to myself as much as possible while the *deliverance process* was allowed to continue. So I kept quiet about things and did not disclose fully to people what we were experiencing.

It finally came time for my mother to leave for Africa. I did all that was laid in my heart to do on her behalf. I bought several types

---

8   2 Corinthians 2:11.

of things for her and filled suitcases with new clothes in addition to what she already had. I purchased many more undergarments for her as well as toiletries. I made sure she had everything I could think she would need.

I had been warned by the lead pastor to not let my mother know she would be leaving for Freetown. A few of the pastors shared stories about how they had been receiving attacks following every one of our deliverance meetings. So they were concerned not only for me and my daughter but also for themselves. And the lead pastor pointed out that my family's issues were "severe."

He said, "The forces involved are powerful."

The day before my mother was scheduled to leave for Freetown, I arranged for my mother to join Camilla and me in spending the night at my friend's place. I left my mother at my friend's home in the morning and told her I was coming back to pick her up in a few hours.

Not wanting to pack all of my mother's things by myself, I enlisted my sister-friend to help me—sharing with her only that I needed her help at home on that particular day. After dropping my daughter off at school, my friend helped me pack all of my mother's belongings in suitcases and one carry on piece of luggage.

While packing, I told my friend I was sending my mother back home and why I was doing it. I decided to not give her more information than necessary so I wouldn't need to get into all the details of the bigger picture. That's how I handled it. And she did not insist on needing to know more about our family business.

After we had all of my mother's things packed, I encouraged my friend to head back to her house ahead of me since I didn't want my mother to know she had been my helper. I wanted to spare her any retaliation. As time drew near for my mother to leave for the airport, I headed back to my friend's place and helped my mother get ready to leave.

I had arranged for an *Uber* driver to pick up my mother while I drove alone to the airport. That was what the lead pastor had advised me to do. The *Uber* car arrived, and I loaded my mother's bags into the trunk. Then I informed my mother that I would meet her at the airport.

I sobbed like a child. My friend tried to console me but to no avail. I could not control myself. My emotions were all over the place.

I and the *Uber* driver arrived at the airport together. I unloaded my mother's bags and ensured she was checked in and ready for her flight. I also gave her some money for her expenses for at least a few months. I then told my mother for the first time the reason why I was sending her back home to Freetown. I cited what had happened and her defiance to receiving help.

I told my mother she had been unwilling to share what she knew and had not been genuinely receptive to the process of helping us deal with our struggles and afflictions. Her eyes watered up as I fought back my own tears.

I gently hugged her before she made her way through security. I then stood to the side and watched her go through the TSA lines. I began to cry again because I knew she had wasted the opportunity God had provided her—the mercy He had shown her by allowing her to come close to her daughter.

I felt depleted because my mother had chosen darkness over light. What she had pledged either willingly or unwilling had overpowered her and put her in a position of fear. I mourned because she had trampled upon the salvation of our Lord Jesus

Christ that had been freely given to her, and she had done it with a level of indifference that pierced my heart.

I waved my very last waves to her and walked off without looking back. I prayed that God would grant her safe arrival. I cried as I drove back to my friend's place. The lead pastor called as I was driving back to see if my mother had left for Freetown. In bitter agony, I shared with him what transpired. He then encouraged me to cheer up. And I told him I would.

But talk is cheap. Our situation was not a small matter that could easily be brushed off. Life was not suddenly going to snap back to normal. There was still a battle left behind for me to fight.

I was told that battle was indeed mine to fight because of ancestral practices that still today empowers dark forces within my family. Clearly, I didn't understand enough about it. Nor did I know what to do except follow the directions of the pastors and look to the One whom I knew was always faithful.

Look to the LORD and His strength; seek his face always.
(1 Chronicles 16:11)

CHAPTER 8

Uphold Me, and I Will Be Delivered [9]

In you, Lord, I have taken refuge; let me never be put to shame; deliver me in your righteousness.   (Psalm 31:1)

THERE CAME A time when the attacks on my daughter and me became very severe, so the lead pastor advised that I terminate my relationship with my mother and siblings for a while and focus on my daughter and me. I agreed with him that my family and I could rekindle our relationship at a later time. So I did as he advised.

---

9   Psalm 119:117.

Now if you thought all our problems were going to disappear when my mother returned to Africa, you were wrong. In some ways our troubles only increased. If you remember the beginning of my story you will know the things that introduced me to the spiritual battle my daughter and I were engaged in had already started before my mother arrived.

Dealing with my mother gave us some insight into the battle but didn't end it. After she left, the battle actually only intensified.

My body was no longer my own. My daughter and I began living with an uninvited and unwanted companion—a black shadowy figure that looked like a spider web that followed me around all the time. And I still ached all over and was in discomfort with constant crawling and moving sensations in my body. My daughter also began experiencing some of the same unpleasant sensations.

Our lives increasingly became riddled with uncertainty, with neither of us having an adequate solution for it.

But we were not about to give up to the forces that battled against us. The psalmist, Ethan the Ezrahite, wrote, *"Righteousness and justice are the foundation of Your throne"* (Psalm 89:14a AMP). I thought about my history with God and how through His providence He had continued to walk faithfully with me. So without reservation, I was still resolute in surrendering everything to Him and trusting in His infinite mercy and grace as we lived our lives day by day trusting in the Lord's *righteousness and justice.*

My daughter and I continued to rely on the support and guidance of the pastors from the non-denominational church. And my sister-friend became an asset we could not have done without. A change was also occurring through which it appeared that God himself arrested our lives—meaning the outside world became almost non-existent or irrelevant to us.

I was not big on going out and engaging in many social activities anyway, but what I'm talking about was on a whole other level. My daughter and I only engaged in church-related activities. Watching television was completely removed from our desires and replaced by more time pursuing spiritual insights.

I had learned more about how to worship God with song. And even though I am not a great singer, He was equipping me with a spiritual weapon. So in receiving that which I was seeking from God, singing His praises and being in His presence were two of the greatest gifts among all the others He bestowed on me. It seemed I was being stripped of my old self—that is, except for what was still a mystery in my body and my surroundings.

The pastors voiced their concerns with me because nothing changed in spite of all the prayer and fasting. But because of how God had carried my daughter and me through the perils and trials we had already faced, I was unmoved by their position. The roles were becoming reversed as I became the one who most emphasized God's Power and ability to see my daughter and me through the storm.

I had received a level of confidence that only the Good Lord could have given me. So I was determined to tackle each day as it came with confidence in the power of God. But with the enemy knowing my position—that I was like the three Hebrew men faced with the furnace,[10] defiant and uncompromising in allegiance to God—his attacks became even more severe.

---

10 Daniel chapter three.

I could feel physical changes in my body that came and went each day. And I recognized my mind was slipping further away into the unknown. But I kept most of those things to myself out of concern I would trouble my daughter and the pastors. But even so, I believe my daughter was aware that something was drastically wrong with me mentally.

Thoughts of suicide began to occupy me again. Nevertheless, I used what God had given me a few months earlier to reaffirm what I knew. Worship kept my thoughts centered on God.

King David wrote, *"I will praise God's name in song and glorify him with thanksgiving"* (Psalm 69:30). David knew the power of praise. As the days became harder and harder for him, worship and praise became his food and water. And for me it became the same. Physical food no longer felt like a necessity, because I had little appetite for it.

The significance in the Messiah's words recorded in the book of Matthew specifically stood out and became profound to me at that time.

> *But Jesus replied, "It is written and forever remains written, 'MAN SHALL NOT LIVE BY BREAD ALONE, BUT BY EVERY WORD THAT COMES OUT OF THE MOUTH OF GOD.'"*
>
> (Matthew 4:4 AMP)

My body needed food and water to survive, but what had been an attack in my body had slowly carved away my appetite. With that, however, I found a greater appreciation for what the Bible says. Paul wrote to the Christians in Rome and said:

> *For whatever was written in earlier times was written for our instruction so that through endurance and the encouragement of*

the Scriptures we might have hope and overflow with confidence
in His promises. (Romans 15:4 AMP)

Even though Paul wrote those words nearly two thousand years ago, both his words and all the other words in the Bible that he referred to as having been written in even earlier times—even over a thousand years earlier than Paul's writing—were written for us. It was all written to instruct us and to provide to us the spiritual food we desperately need.

My daughter and I went for several more deliverance sessions as recommended by the lead pastor. Those sessions were with the pastor who had confronted my mother regarding my childhood. The pastor advised us to fast a few days before each session, which my daughter and I did. One thing I liked about that pastor was that he worshiped a lot. Also, he read Scriptures from the Bible when ministering to us and used less of all the other gestures (such as the tapping of the forehead).

We spent a few hours with him during each session. When they ended I left with expectations that God was answering our prayers. And I encouraged Camilla not to think differently in fear of introducing any form of unbelief into her mind. To ensure my encouragement was successful, I opened dialogues with her about the many great things God had done for us and gave her specific examples. With that approach, I knew her fears would subside while her trust in God increased.

My daughter knows several significant Bible verses, particularly those in the Psalms that illustrate the truth about God, His Power, and our position as His children. I often asked her to read out loud a Psalm that applied in her moments of despair. She also had become accustomed to praying and fasting, and she had learned how to worship—all of which I encouraged her to do on her own in addition to us two doing it collectively.

Paul, while encouraging his spiritual son, wrote to Timothy, *"You have been taught the holy Scriptures from childhood, and they have given you the wisdom to receive the salvation that comes by trusting in Christ Jesus"* (2 Timothy 3:15 NLT). It was imperative that I encourage Camilla to apply the Scriptures so she would have the same wisdom Timothy had been given.

Eventually, the lead pastor at the non-denominational church advised me to stop attending the Catholic church, which we did. I believed that they were not diminishing the doctrine of the Catholic Church. Instead, they were aware of our predicament and knew that we needed a more intense form of prayer and worship.

To replace going to the Adoration Chapel, I started going to a "Prayer House" that the lead pastor suggested. This *Prayer House* is well known across the United States. And like the Adoration Chapel at the Catholic church, the *Prayer House* became a place of refuge for me.

I maintained the same schedule—arriving around 8:30 AM and staying until around 2:30 PM. The atmosphere of live worship and praise provided to me a level of serenity that helped calm the storm. I continued with that routine for several months while believing and trusting God for a break in our circumstances.

But nothing shifted. It seemed to only grow worse. Then I began to sense that the pastors were beginning to grow weary. I felt uneasy and worrisome about what might become of us if the pastors were to abandon us. I began to hear complaints from some that they had never done a deliverance that "lasted as long" as ours. Others continued to say they were "receiving attacks" on account of us that caused them to be "concerned."

It became clear to me that a shift was occurring within the confines of where we had found solace. The truth is, I was naïve, and so I believed those pastors were themselves our lifeline. Therefore, I resorted to being like the psalmist, who when in distress cried unto the Lord, *"Uphold me, and I will be delivered"* (Psalm 119:117a).

In the midst of all that, the lead pastor approached me with yet another plan. That time, he was assigning my daughter and me to one of his associate pastors who had only recently joined the church. That was a plan I was a bit reluctant to comply with because we had gone through so many hands, and I viewed it as counterproductive.

However, the lead pastor assured me that he trusted that associate pastor and that I should trust his authority. So I did (but while quietly screaming inside, "Aiutami!" which is Italian for "Help me!").

So we starting working with that associate pastor, who began to organize a prayer vigil. For about three weeks, the associate pastor scheduled for three other pastors from the church to join him in conducting a weekly night vigil for us to participate in. Those night vigils were held on Friday nights from 8:00 PM until sometimes one or two o'clock on Saturday morning.

That was a totally new experience for me, but I did it since everything that was incorporated into it was biblical—reading of Scriptures and worship, which was in line with what I was already doing. And it turned out that the application of the Scriptures and the way it was presented (by someone who had knowledge, which was something I lacked at the time) caused me to yearn to know more of God.

*Open my eyes [to spiritual truth] so that I may behold Wonderful
things from Your law.*   (Psalm 119:18 AMP)

I began to dream frequently during the time we engaged in
those night vigils. The associate pastor then asked me to write
down my dreams and share them with him, which I did. Because
I dreamed so much, he once remarked, "You are truly connected
to heaven." Of course he didn't know that I have always dreamed,
so it was nothing new for me.

My dreams sometimes contained mysteries that the pastor
could not interpret. So he directed me to pray for dreams he
deemed were "favorable" to come to pass and pray that those that
were "unfavorable and not of God" be canceled. I obeyed and
began praying that way.

Later, the lead pastor approached me one day and said the
associate pastor told him my daughter and I should be "dedicated
to an altar." According to him, the associate pastor's reasoning
was for us to be dedicated to an altar to "counter what my family
allowed to be in place over the years."

I questioned the need for that action and inquired about
what it entailed. The lead pastor shared with me that the
process consisted of prayer and worship, after which a "prayer of
dedication" would be made to God on our behalf. I agreed to go
through with the plan, and I was then asked to do a fast with my
daughter before the dedication.

The day came for the prayer of dedication. It was a Friday.
We arrived at the church at 7:00 PM and met with the associate
pastor. We then began with praise and worship that lasted for
about two hours. Then the associate pastor started the dedication
by inviting us to the altar.

I had been asked to bring a bottle of anointing oil with me to the meeting. The pastor took the bottle of oil, prayed over it, and began pouring it on the top of my head. The oil ran down over my entire body as he prayed. The same was done to my daughter.

The dedication was brief. In the end, my daughter and I were soaked in anointing oil to the point that we could not open our eyes. While struggling to see my way through the church, the associate pastor told us my daughter and I were "no longer bound to what my family worshiped."

You may wonder why I agreed to go through the dedication ceremony if I had already been trusting in God and seeking His guidance (which is valid curiosity on your part). I still today don't have all the answers when it comes to spiritual things. But more importantly, there was even more I didn't understand back then. I also felt responsible for demonstrating a certain level of obedience while under that church's authority.

On the following Sunday afternoon, I had just taken a shower and sat down on the floor at a friend's house, where we had been for the weekend. While sitting there in a still moment of worship, I began to shake uncontrollably. I thought I was having a seizure. I was alert but without control of my entire body. Then it ended suddenly, and I began to sing, "Let the glory of the Lord rise among us." I sang that song and continued to worship with other worship songs until I was myself again.

I was not the same after that incident.

I didn't know what the shaking was about, but I knew it was both preceded by and followed by worship. And looking back, I remembered the time I felt like I was being strangled and how after passing out I awoke quoting Scripture. I felt that neither of those incidents could have been a coincidence, so I shared with the pastor and his associate pastor what had taken place.

When they heard about my shaking and worship, they both assured me that I had "received the Holy Spirit." According to the pastors, it was "the indwelling of the Holy Spirit" that came upon me. One of them said, "God really loves you." Of course that was a truth I had already known because God himself told me that many years earlier.

A few days following that incident, I woke up one morning speaking in an unknown tongue. I woke up with my mouth filled with a language I had never heard or spoken before. The lead pastor was pleased, as the ministry of that church promotes speaking and praying in tongues. He had actually been encouraging me to speak in tongues.

My response to him in the past had been, "In God's timing, that will occur."

He emphasized that, "Praying in tongues is a powerful tool against the enemy."

Well, I will tell you for certain, my experience that morning was absolutely not something I could manufacture on my own. I continued to pray in English until that morning.

The pastor was happy and proclaimed to me that I had "received power to fight the opponent."

As time went on, though, I began to question that pairing with the Spirit of God, as something seemed amiss. I began to speak in those unknown languages that seemed to change every so often. I prayed and sang beautifully in the languages for hours. My days were filled with moments like that. But I was experiencing more than just speaking in other tongues.

I remember one evening when I acted like a lion during one of our night vigils that followed. I displayed a level of aggression while I moved from room to room praying in those languages. At one point, it was as if I flew through the hallway with both of my hands swinging in the air as one brandishing a sword.

All three associate pastors present continued praying and worshiping and showed no concern, which encouraged me to push my reservations aside and believe such episodes were normal. After all, I considered, if there would have been anything wrong with my behavior I assumed the pastors would have caught it and redirected me, but that didn't happen.

So whenever I displayed strange episodes like that, I lived through them continuing to believe they were the manifestation of the Spirit of God. And as I continued to worship "in the Spirit," I soon began prophesying.

There were several things happening at the church that I prophesied accurately about, including personal matters about a few members. The lead pastor approached me and asked me to pray for the members to whom I had given a prophetic message.

One time, I believed I received detailed instructions on what to wear and where to sit in the church on a particular Sunday, because I was going to pray for a specific member of the church. I followed the instructions, but I also consulted with the associate pastor. At prayer time, he stood with me as I prayed with the member. During the prayer, I spoke a revelatory word pertaining to her situation. She jumped up from where we both sat—with the associate pastor standing beside us—and shouted, "It is true!"

I had not spoken to her or with anyone at the church about her before that day, so I had no insight about what the word meant to her.

Earlier, another member, who had received a word that she was going to be healed—just as the associate pastor prophesied during his sermon—approached me and asked me to pray for her. I jumped right into praying with her. And before I knew it, we were locked hand in hand and praying. Then I began to pray in tongues. Unexpectedly, she and I started spinning in a circle until we both came to a complete stop.

That was a familiar episode for me since that also happened to me while I was being delivered. In her case, though, I didn't know what it was about. But at the end of our prayers, I found myself at the altar thanking God for how He had used me that day to minister to those people.

Oh, the mercy of God!

But You, O Lord, are a God of compassion and mercy, slow to get angry and filled with unfailing love and faithfulness.

(Psalm 86:15 NLT)

Only God could restrain himself so from judging us for what we have done and instead pour out to us blessing after blessing.

I became a hot commodity to the church with my newly acquired "spiritual gift." The associate pastor often called on me to pray for certain church members who were facing some spiritual attacks. And as I prayed for them I often received a word through prophecy that I shared with the lead pastor and the associate pastor.

The lead pastor, however, seemed a bit hesitant to accept all that I was becoming. I remember I once prophesied about a person who was going through a huge challenge. I spoke with considerable insight into her problems without ever having spoken to her or a pastor or anyone else at the church about her.

The lead pastor received the prophecy, but I could see his level of curiosity about how I could be so precise with the revelations I was receiving when I had been baptized with the gift of the Holy Spirit for only a short time.

Nonetheless, I was soon included in a prayer team with those who prayed for members who were "afflicted." But on the back end, my daughter and I were still experiencing our own problems.

There was another pastor who lives outside of the United States, to whom the lead pastor had introduced me, and I had been praying with him as well. We had a good rapport because he also prayed with me using Scriptures. Not long after I had been praying with him, he called to tell me the Lord had asked him to allow his sister to pray with me too. His sister was to become the only other woman who would be part of our prayer group. I welcomed what he said and began praying with his sister.

I must say that up until then I had never heard anyone pray like she prayed. She appeared to command authority when she prayed and seemed to know the direction in which she should focus her prayers. I had never prayed like that before. My own prayers were direct and simple based on what I believed was in my heart to pray for and nothing associated with "warfare prayers," which is what she called the kinds of prayers she prayed.

When we prayed together, I felt like an elementary student in the school of prayer; that's how intensely she prayed. She and I quickly bonded and developed a sisterhood. She said that she, too, had experienced some spiritual warfare due to "generational strongholds" in her family. And she also had been to several deliverance meetings where she had learned to pray like she did. Therefore, she understood what my daughter and I were experiencing.

One afternoon I was on my knees praying during our prayer session with the pastor outside of the U.S. and his sister. Suddenly, I let out the loudest scream I have ever heard in my life and was thrown to the floor face down. I was conscious and could still hear my prayer partners praying, but I could not move. Also, I sensed the presence of a man standing at the end of my feet saying something over me, but I could not make out what he was saying.

I laid flat on my stomach, unable to look up, while the person spoke over me for what seemed like a very long time, which in fact it was. My prayer partners continued to pray as that was taking place until I could get up from the floor. The pastor asked if the presence of the man was threatening. I responded, "No."

Then he said, "It was the Holy Spirit."

We ended our prayer with thanksgiving after once again having been visited by the third person of the Trinity. There seemed to be agreement that I had received a double dose of the Holy Spirit.

But had I?

What followed that experience left me questioning some behaviors and spiritual manifestations.

The Bible speaks to the issue of false spirits. And in First Thessalonians 5:20-21, we read, *"Do not scoff at prophecies, but test everything that is said. Hold on to what is good"* (NLT). That means it is not necessary for us to believe the things people prophesy as God inspired just because they said it came from God. We are supposed to put it to the test.

Also, by studying Scripture I came to understand that even people appointed by God and used by Him could be led astray into error. And I realized that everyone seemed perfectly comfortable with my "spiritual gifts" even though some things about them seemed strange to me. So I determined to assume the position of judging myself.

Nonetheless, I continued to prophesy and speak and sing in tongues, because those gifts continued to flow whenever they would and without me initiating it. My prayer life eventually consisted of mostly praying in tongues. But then things began to change.

I realized that our situation was not getting better but instead growing worse. Then I began prophesying about things related to what my mother had done and how that affected me. Specific information began to pour in to me sometimes on a minute-by-minute basis. Honestly, I was being overloaded with information about what my mother had presumably done to me as a child.

But the revelations weren't limited to my mother alone but also to what some of my siblings did against me. It was wild! I didn't know what to make of it, so I started recording those messages and sending them to the lead pastor, and I sought his advice.

I was overwhelmed at the rate at which I was prophesying and with the level of accuracy at which the prophecies came. Interestingly, though, the lead pastor's attitude then started to change toward me. In fact, the attitudes of all of the pastors who had been working with my daughter and me started changing (but not the attitudes of the pastor and his sister who lived out of the country).

I didn't know any better, so I did my best to continue in my obedience to the pastors and the church. I didn't know where else to go, and I didn't know who else could explain such mysteries to me since those manifestations began while under the supervision of that church.

The pastors, however, soon appeared to care less about where I had found myself with my "Spirit gifts." I could sense that I had become a burden to them, particularly to the lead pastor, who didn't seem to know where I should belong in the whole scheme of things. On one hand, he questioned me about the origin of the prophecies, but on the other hand, it seemed to me he gladly used revelations from the prophecies freely anytime it was convenient for him and members of the church.

I already had my reservations about all of it, so I firmly concluded that something was very wrong. Needless to say, I knew I needed to put an end to my relationship with members of that church. My daughter and I stopped attending, but we did not leave in strife. I didn't want to burn my bridges with any of them because of how I felt.

I didn't have all of the answers, but I held on to my belief that if God continued to uphold me—support me and keep me from sinking—I would eventually be delivered from all my enemies, even those at work in my mind.

I tried to apply wisdom, and I did my best to make an informed decision that would not displease God. But regardless, I needed the blessed assurance that God was still going to walk with me.

When you go through deep waters,
   I will be with you.
When you go through rivers of difficulty,
   you will not drown.
When you walk through the fire of oppression,
   you will not be burned up;
   the flames will not consume you.
                                             (Isaiah 43:2 NLT)

CHAPTER 9

What God Has Joined Together

But whoever is united with the Lord is one with him in spirit.
(1 Corinthians 6:17)

WHILE JESUS WAS in the region of Judea ministering to the people, some Pharisees approached him to test him. The ever-tricky Pharisees were always looking for something they could use to trip up Jesus and give them something to use against him.

They asked him about the marriage laws established by Moses. And Jesus answered them without hesitation.

"Is it lawful for a man to divorce his wife?" they asked Jesus.

"What did Moses command you?" he replied.

They said, "Moses permitted a man to write a certificate of divorce and send her away."

"It was because your hearts were hard that Moses wrote you this law," Jesus replied. "But at the beginning of creation God 'made them male and female.' 'For this reason a man will leave his father and mother and be united to his wife, and the two will become one flesh.' So they are no longer two, but one flesh. Therefore what God has joined together, let no one separate." (Mark 10:2-9)

What Jesus said was direct and straight to the point. This conversation in the Bible has served for centuries as a seal that declares the marriage covenant between a man and a woman.

Undoubtedly, the words of Jesus quoted above refer to an earthly marriage between a man and a woman. But the forever-bond between a husband and wife is also used in Scripture to illustrate the bond between Jesus and the Church. And even as recorded in the Old Testament, God's people were presented as having such a bond to God. They were compared to an unfaithful spouse when they became disloyal to God.[11]

Now, today, like all of God's people who lived before us, each one of us bears a level of accountability in the Church's relationship to her Bridegroom. People often talk about forces that come against us—strongholds, afflictions, Satan, devils, demons, evil spirits, and other things—as being responsible for all our troubles. But frequently when it comes to our tendencies to yield to temptation and fall into error, the culprit to blame for the results lies not without but within. Both personally and corporately, believers all too often secretly grant invitations to the opposition to cause trouble and confusion.

And like the people of God described in the Old Testament, believers today all too often yield to temptation, make bad decisions, dismiss their responsibilities, and just satisfy themselves

---

11 Ezekiel chapter sixteen contains one of the more vivid analogies.

with the broken pieces of their fractured union with God. But continuing that eventually leads to ruin. So why continue such a life when we have a Bridegroom who loves like no other?

Jeremiah spoke to God's people in bondage and captivity.

The LORD appeared to us in the past, saying: "I have loved you with an everlasting love; I have drawn you with unfailing kindness. I will build you up again." (Jeremiah 31:3-4a)

Sadly, in my time of peril I discovered that I had neglected the importance of my bridal duty to the Bridegroom. I had made bad decisions, but I continued to believe, hold on to, and place my hope in God's *unfailing kindness.*

I came to the awareness that I knew very little about Him—the One who has always loved me. Even though I had been dedicated to Him during my Baptism, First Holy Communion, and then at Confirmation, and even though I thought I had done my best to love Him since He captivated me through His providence, I didn't really *know* Him.

You see, I have been what I felt was a devoted Christian with an almost perfect church attendance record. But the truth is, like so many others in the same or similar positions, *I never truly loved Him with all my heart.* What do I mean by this? Let me explain how I feel about it now.

When we love our spouses, children, family members, or others, we establish special places for them in our hearts. We give our best for them, and we let them know by our actions that they are valued and loved. They are given proper places among all our relationships with others. And I had not given God His proper place.

The vast majority of what really loving Him means was missing from our relationship. And that's because I hadn't learned what God's proper place in my life is supposed to be.

I believed what I had become for Him was all He required. I had vowed to live a disciplined life, one that is free from sin. I loved my neighbors as myself. (Well . . . I tried!) You get the idea. But after leaving the non-denominational church, I started listening to the messages of many great men and women of God—many of whom have gone to be with the Lord. And as I learned from their teachings, I became more aware of my faults.

Eventually I realized I knew little to nothing about the Bridegroom and God who created me, who had sustained me, and whose mercy had kept my daughter and me from being devoured by the enemy.

But I assure you, I was not angry at the world or with those to whom I had previously entrusted my spiritual life—and that of my daughter. Instead, I was angry because I had failed to dig deep into the Bible to read and understand words such as these:

> So Jesus was saying to the Jews who had believed Him, "If you abide in My word [continually obeying My teachings and living in accordance with them, then] you are truly My disciples. And you will know the truth [regarding salvation], and the truth will set you free [from the penalty of sin]." (John 8:31-32 AMP)

Here is an assurance from the Bridegroom himself that should have caused me to take a road less traveled. I became brokenhearted at what I had missed for so long.

One day as I sat in a room with my daughter, I began to yearn to know more of God—to gain answers for all the things I didn't understand about what we had been going through. I then realized the first thing I needed to do to get the answers I desired was to seek God in a profound way, as I had never done before.

I read in Jeremiah where God said:

Then [with a deep longing] you will seek Me and require Me [as a vital necessity] and [you will] find Me when you search for Me with all your heart.   (Jeremiah 29:13 AMP)

And I read the words of Jesus, who said:

But the Helper (Comforter, Advocate, Intercessor—Counselor, Strengthener, Standby), the Holy Spirit, whom the Father will send in My name [in My place, to represent Me and act on My behalf], He will teach you all things. And He will help you remember everything that I have told you.   *(John 14:26 AMP)*

So I became more and more aware that the Holy Spirit had partnered with me and was instructing me in the ways of the Father. And I became more thankful that the Lord had given to me my relationship with the pastor and his sister who are out of the country. Through their counsel, I went back to the beginning to pursue Scripture and not simply base truth on what I had been told by others.

Up until then, I had relied on going to church, reading the Bible *verses of the day,* and at times even writing them down in hopes of studying them again. Don't get me wrong, I read the Bible, knew of Scriptures, and could recite those I had fallen in love with. But there was a huge lack on my part in ensuring that my role as a member of the Bride of Christ fulfilled the expectations of the Groom.

My relationship with God had been centered on prayer, worship, fasting, and listening to spiritual messages—and that was all good. And I had remained a faithful giver in giving the church my tithes, time, and talents. But I didn't come close to studying the Word of God as I should have to actually develop the kind of relationship with God I needed.

I must say, my time in Bible reading was severely lacking or ill-developed. I am talking about studying the Bible to develop a deep-rooted knowledge of God's Word—investing one-on-one time with the Lord. In that, I was deficient. I didn't even come close to understanding the passion of the psalmist who wrote, *"Thy word is a lamp unto my feet, and a light unto my path"* (Psalm 119:105 KJV).

Now, through both experience and study, I have found that to know all of God is to understand that His Word doesn't just guide us along the paths we are to walk in. It also illuminates the paths we should avoid in order to prevent us from becoming victims of the pitfalls of this world and the enemies of our souls.

My serious study of the Bible provided to me a fresh light into the full sovereignty of God's character, His laws, principles, warnings, grace, mercies, promises, and more. As I read the Bible from the book of Genesis through the book of Revelation, I came to accept that I previously hadn't known anything at all.

It became true that *"the unfolding of your words gives light; it gives understanding to the simple"* (Psalm 119:130).

There began the renewing of our vows—not so much by Him, as He is the same forever, but rather by me. I began to fall in love as one smitten by a man whose good looks causes me to gasp in admiration. But the truth is, I was not in awe of merely One, but rather with the entire Trinity, who was in full display.

I was mesmerized by the truth of the Father, who gave His only begotten Son, the Son, who died for my sins, and the Holy Spirit, who was sent to me to abide with me and guide me throughout life. My heart melted at the beauties of God's creation. I marveled at His supremacy.

And as I continued to be enthralled by the mighty power of God during my one-on-one time studying His Word, I found that I was beginning to be lured into an aroma so pure that it actually purified my heart. It was as if the exquisite nature of God was illuminating my understanding to know of His divine electricity that charges the hearts of His children when they make themselves available to Him.

Then I realized that ours is a love story that deserves its place on every stage, but I also realized that I had a responsibility to share the magnificent treasure I had found.

I had discovered a love story that is not to be hidden. To the contrary, it should be shouted from the rooftop. It deserves an audience with a listening ear that has been opened by the gentle hand of the Holy Spirit. It is a love story so divine and unique that one is left unfulfilled if it is not cultivated—which suggests that one doesn't honestly know what love is about until the seed of that love is planted.

I then thought of Jesus' words in Matthew.

Take My yoke upon you and learn from Me [following Me as My disciple], for I am gentle and humble in heart, and YOU WILL FIND REST (renewal, blessed quiet) FOR YOUR SOULS. For My yoke is easy [to bear], and My burden is light.
(Matthew 11:29-30 AMP)

Then came the realization that I must not set any other standard by which I must live my life except by the Word of

God. I formed a conclusion that I cannot pick and choose which part of God's Word I should read and study. And as I learned the breathtaking truth of my Lord, I found I was naked without any tools to use in handling the blows of the enemy if I stood alone.

Alone, I didn't have the knowledge required to be my arsenal for success before going into the battlefield. Paul wrote, *"For the weapons of our warfare are not carnal, but mighty through God to the pulling down of strong holds"* (2 Corinthians 10:4 KJV).

In time, it dawned on me that a child of God must not rely only on the teachings of his or her pastor, mentors, Bible study sessions, and the likes. While all those sources are genuinely valuable and proper, I could see that the knowledge we need to be victorious in every area of our lives cannot be attained through those alone. We need to know God's Word ourselves.

There are too many unforeseen battles to fight. The world is too full of evil. Moreover, as my own life testifies, some of us have family backgrounds that have exposed us to the wiles and deception of the enemy.

Make no mistake, none of us is immune to the wickedness and temptations of the enemy. But neither are we alone without God understanding our situations.

Jesus had fasted forty days and forty nights when He *"was led by the Spirit into the wilderness to be tempted by the devil."* There, Jesus himself showed a certain dependance on the Word of God to counter His tempter by quoting Scripture and declaring, *"It is written."* [12]

Jesus set the standard for us by being properly equipped to face temptation. And Paul instructed us about the importance of God's Word when dealing with spiritual battles.

---

12 Matthew 4:1-10.

A final word: Be strong in the Lord and in his mighty power. Put on all of God's armor so that you will be able to stand firm against all strategies of the devil. For we are not fighting against flesh-and-blood enemies, but against evil rulers and authorities of the unseen world, against mighty powers in this dark world, and against evil spirits in the heavenly places.

Therefore, put on every piece of God's armor so you will be able to resist the enemy in the time of evil. Then after the battle you will still be standing firm. Stand your ground, putting on the belt of truth and the body armor of God's righteousness. For shoes, put on the peace that comes from the Good News so that you will be fully prepared. In addition to all of these, hold up the shield of faith to stop the fiery arrows of the devil. Put on salvation as your helmet, and take the sword of the Spirit, which is the word of God

(Ephesians 6:10-17 NLT)

The Word of God and faith in His Word equip and guide us. They keep us from stumbling when we are tempted to live contrary to God's plans for His beloved sons and daughters.

My daughter and I could have been dead for lack of knowledge if it were not for the grace of God. By only God's grace, we found Scripture to be a weapon. The Book of Life became more to us than simply a revered book to display in our home. It indeed became our arsenal standing against the weapons of the enemy and his cohorts as we relied upon it for our daily walk with God.

God had joined us together with Christ, and with God's love and compassion for us—with God's Word in our hearts—we were determined to not be separated from Him.

CHAPTER 10

The Seven Day Journey

At the end of that time, I, Nebuchadnezzar, raised my eyes toward heaven, and my sanity was restored. Then I praised the Most High; I honored and glorified him who lives forever.

(Daniel 4:34) [13]

AT THIS POINT you probably feel like I finally got my act together and my terrible experience battling against the powers of darkness was over. But although I paused in my story to tell you about what I learned of God's truth in so many ways, I still had a long way to go.

My battle with the enemy, and my struggle to overcome the effects of my past and the past decisions and influences of my

---

13 Nebuchadnezzar had spent "seven times" in a state of insanity. See Daniel chapter four to read of Nebuchadnezzar's dream and what followed it.

family, were far from over. So for your benefit, and to my regret, I must sojourn into the irrefutable truth about what I call my and Camilla's *seven day journey.*

As many people have explained in many ways, the number *seven* is significant, or prominent, in the Bible. I have heard it said that *seven* is the scriptural number of perfection or completion. So it seems ironic, but perhaps actually fitting, that there was a period of seven days in which my daughter and I were catapulted from the realm of the normal into the abnormal.

Because of our experiences during those seven days, I have decided to coin the number *seven* as a *number of awakening* for me.

Truly, an awakening, or as I present it in this book, a transformation, was to be in my future. But before I could realize the power and miracle of my spiritual metamorphosis, I first had to spend seven days that I can only describe in a few words as a cocoon of terror.

I honestly cannot pinpoint the exact time our lives spiraled out of control during those seven days, but it finally did. I had already stopped going to the non-denominational church where things began to drastically change for me. But after leaving the church, the lead pastor asked for a meeting one day, and during the meeting he recommended that I visit with another pastor friend of his for yet another session of prayer and deliverance.

He told me that, "because things had progressed in a downward spiral," that new pastor was trained and could help me further.

When I declined, he became upset and terminated my affiliation with the church. Well, I had already stopped going, so that did not bother me. But I wondered about how I had surrendered our lives to those pastors and entrusted our care so thoroughly into their hands.

There are many things that took place between us and those pastors during that time that I have chosen to not write about— even as I have not written about all of the things I learned about my family. God was, and still is, privy to all of it, and He will judge accordingly.

By then, I was on the precipice of experiencing unkind changes comprised of both unusual physical experiences and a mind that sometimes seemed to function without my control. I had a level of energy that I could not explain. Granted, I had been told on two separate occasions that I had received the "Holy Spirit's baptism." But by then my prayer life consisted almost entirely of me "speaking in tongues."

I often prayed for hours in *tongues* without an ounce of fatigue. There were days when I went without any sleep yet was still alert and active. By that, I mean I went for days on end praying in tongues and reading the Bible and other motivational books I had purchased. It was also during that time when many prophecies were coming from my mouth like a stream of water flowing through its canal.

I actually began prophesying to myself about my own life and person, and the prophecies seemed like very strange revelations. I called another pastor who had been introduced to me a short time earlier and inquired about the progression of my "gifts." He, too, assured me my gifts were from God. And he continued to say that, "Often, when God begins to use a person, the enemy also attempts to introduce himself with manipulations, so you should pray and not worry."

That, however, seemed like conflicting information to me because of something that had transpired at the church I had been attending. The lead pastor once told me that my gifts were a result of a "spirit of divination." And that came mere weeks after he and a few of his associate pastors assured me that I had received the gift of the Holy Spirit baptism.

But in spite of that, the pastor often used the prophecy I had delivered in the church as it pertained to the church members with such a level of conviction that the message had surely come directly from God.

Should anyone wonder why sometimes I might have been in a state of confusion?

Undoubtedly, one thing for sure, I knew something was amiss, but I didn't know what. The level of energy I felt after that was at its peak. I then began to prophesy about my future, particularly of the great wealth and destiny that awaited me. But one day as I was going through what had by that time become my daily routine, a revelation came to me that sent me into a level of fear that I had never experienced.

It was on that day when our seven day journey into the unknown began.

I began experiencing a powerful fear, and I was so fearful that I decided my daughter and I should spend the night at our neighbor's place. But I couldn't get them on the phone, so Camilla and I got in the car with the hope of spending the night in a hotel.

We left our home to spend the night in a hotel, but I ended up driving all night around the streets of nearby towns. It was unreal! And, yes, it was bizarre of me to decide to do that. And I couldn't even explain then why I was doing it, but for some reason, it seemed like the thing I should do.

I wish I could tell you now that my strange behavior stopped the following morning. I wish I could say that our lives returned to the way it was before that level of fear entered my mind, but I can't say it. For sadly, driving around different cities and places became a routine for us over the next seven days. Those were clearly the darkest of moments for us.

Soon I began to hear a ticking sound that seemed to be following us, and I began seeing things that weren't there. But my mind was so far gone in those moments that everything happening in my mind was a reality to me. What was unreal became real, and what was normal became a threat.

It was then that all of nature seemed to be against me. And eventually even the paved roads were no longer just roads but some displays of frightening objects presented to me as threats to both my mind and body.

I actually attempted to go home several times during those seven days. But each time we arrived home and pulled into the driveway, my mind told me there was danger there, so I backed out of the driveway and drove away to continue what had become an aimless, endless road trip.

While driving around, we attempted to stay in several hotels, but each time we tried, I started hearing the same ticking sound. I especially remember one night when we rented a room in a nearby hotel that was not far from our home. When we arrived, I explained to the front desk attendant that we needed a room but that no one should know we were there. I told him we were being followed, so our identity should be kept a secret.

You have to understand; that was my reality at the time. I was functioning under what was by all accounts my true state of mind. That is, I'm telling you exactly how I felt about the reality I was living in.

My daughter and I had reduced our wardrobe to only a few sets of clothes and a pair of sneakers we purchased from a local store. Everything we had with us over those seven days was in a backpack and a couple of plastic bags holding our dirty clothes. I looked disheveled and out of place. And when I talked to the attendant of the hotel while checking in, I could tell the attendant was alarmed and had concluded that I was mentally off.

I received his demeanor toward us as rude and abnormal. And I was offended by the way he handled us. But at the same time, I was too busy to be too concerned about what the attendant thought. For as we were conducting business I was scouting out the lobby for the culprit who I believed—believed with my entire being—was a threat and in pursuit of us.

Then I happened to look up at the attendant, whose eyes were then fixed intently on me. I could tell he didn't want us to stay there. But he didn't have a choice, because I could afford to pay for the room.

After about twenty minutes, he handed me the keys to a room. I assumed his delay and slow manner of checking us in was an attempt to have me leave on my own accord. But I couldn't; we needed to rest. We had been in the car driving through different cities for a total of eighteen hours non-stop except to use the restroom and to buy my daughter something to eat.

As we made our way upstairs to the hotel room, my mind led me to believe we needed to take off our shoes and hide them somewhere downstairs because they, too, were then presenting a threat to me. I asked my daughter to take off her sneakers as I did mine, and I hid them behind a bench next to an elevator in the lobby and walked upstairs barefooted.

But that's not all of the bizarre actions I took that night (for some reason, I remember it all very well). Once in the room, my mind told me I should cover the mirror and toilet seat, so I took the bed sheets and draped one over the mirror and another over the toilet. I was also led to turn on the shower. Then I lay down, hoping to sleep.

My daughter was in bed, exhausted. I could see that she had begun to fall asleep when, suddenly, I heard a distinctive sound like that of a clock ticking in the room. At that, my mind sensed danger, so I woke up my daughter, gathered the few items we had, and raced out the door.

But we did not leave the hotel before my mind told me I should take off the clothes I was wearing. So I stripped off my clothes in the middle of the hotel hallway and hid them somewhere in the corner of the corridor. I then got another set of clothes from the backpack, put them on, and left.

My daughter stood nearby, watching me with a look of disbelief in her eyes. We raced downstairs, and I told the same attendant that we could not stay because the *threat* had found us. By my actions, I had surely proven his initial assessment of me. He then said to me, "I will process you a refund."

The hotel, however, ended up charging me for the night, and I disputed the charge after later finding out. But during the dispute process, I came to learn what the attendant wrote about me in his nightly report. Here it is:

I strongly believe that this lady has mental issues. Housekeeping reported that the mirror and toilet were covered with sheets. They had taken a shower and left the water running all night.

In his nightly note, the attendant had written down what his face and demeanor had already said to me as he struggled to check us in. And he clearly was not far off base in his initial assessment.

After leaving the hotel that night we continued to drive around town until it was seven o'clock in the morning. As I continued to drive I watched my daughter's tired body slumped on the passenger seat as we drove throughout the night unable to do anything different because of my seriously altered reality.

Don't stop reading now! The insanity gets better (or worse, that is).

As we continued that ridiculous routine, my mind began to direct me to visit homes of people I know. Those men and women have a tremendous amount of respect for me. And I'm pretty sure that the threat I was trying to avoid wanted those men and women to see me in a state of derangement.

But then again, perhaps the Lord wanted them to become aware of my plight, because God in time used them to help me— but more about that later.

Eventually we started going to my sister-friend's place first thing each morning to shower, wash our clothes, and for my daughter to rest. However, at nighttime, we could not stay at her place because I began to experience some of the same strange things in her home like everywhere else.

I continued to be restless and unable to sleep. And when I tried staying at my friend's place I was moved to do all sorts of strange things, such as pacing from door to door, and going from room to room praying in tongues. I also posted myself by her bedroom door all throughout the night as a guard and did more strange things that I won't take the time to describe.

I admit it was absolutely weird. And frankly, I don't have the right words even now to describe all that transpired in the night when we attempted to stay at her place. Strangely, we had visited her home on many occasions and had even called it our second home. But during those days of chaos, we could only stay in my friend's home until around mid-afternoon. Then we continued with driving through different cities until late in the night with no real destination.

Then one night I called another friend and asked if we could spend the night at her place after having driven all day. We were told we could, so my daughter and I went there, arriving late in the night.

Having the belief in my mind that all of nature was against me, I was afraid because that friend lives where many trees and bushes lead to her home. I had developed a coping mechanism when we drove past those kind of areas. I had my daughter cover her face, and sometimes I had her bend low in the front seat, almost to the floor. I then did my best to shield my face and not look at the trees—trusting that I was driving the right way.

During those seven days I also drove without looking in the mirror since to me that also presented a threat. There was something about looking behind me at any time that caused me much fear, because when I did, I saw different objects that I felt were attempting to blind me.

My friend's welcome as we arrived at her home was like others, but I could tell she and her niece, who was staying with her, felt something was very off with me. My outfit was one I ordinarily never would have worn but had become my new runway look—a pair of leggings paired with a black t-shirt, black tennis shoes, and a colorful bandanna on my head.

My friend gave me a concerned look but did not say a word to question my behavior. She was polite and asked if we were OK. Then she offered us something to eat. My daughter was eager to have a home-cooked meal. Afterward, she showed us the room where we would stay the night.

Once in the room we set our things in a corner and planned on taking a shower. The bedroom was carpeted. And as I looked down on the floor, I began to see that the carpet was creating designs that looked similar to the snake-shaped pattern I sometimes saw. Then a level of fear that had gripped me at home came over me again.

That night became one like in a horror movie. I tucked my daughter in tightly between blankets while I lay in bed feeling frantic. Everywhere I looked, I could see the pattern all around the floor of the room. Then I began to hear that ticking sound coming from around me again. It was like it was playing a cat and mouse game with me.

I was discreet, for I didn't want my friend to know what I was experiencing in her home. And finally, in the midst of all that, I drifted off to sleep. But after only a brief time of sleep I awoke to what felt like someone cutting the back of both of my heels with a razor blade. With that, I quickly jumped up, grabbed my daughter from the bed, and took her downstairs.

Once in the living room, I found my friend lying on the couch, sound asleep. I woke her up, presented my daughter to her, and asked that she remain with her until morning. I could tell I had startled my friend, but it was a matter of great importance to do what I did—important to me at least.

I continued trying to conceal from my friend what was going on in my mind as I made my way back upstairs. As I climbed the stairs, the carpet in the hallway leading to the room had the same pattern as the bedroom. And as I looked at it, it left me with such a level of fear that I was unable to move. I stood on the steps, shaking, until I mustered the strength to go into the room. I then quickly grabbed our things and headed downstairs, where I remained until morning without falling asleep.

Something else then began happening that tormented me. It seemed like everything that looked like a string, cord, or even a strand of hair, began looking like a snake to me. Also, my body began to itch and ache as my daughter and I awoke with bruises on our faces and black puffy bags under our eyes. By looking at us, anyone could have easily assumed we were in some kind of abusive relationship and had received a beating from our abuser.

My heels were then burning like someone had washed them in a pot of water mixed with habanero pepper. Then I began to notice that everything I sat on produced a level of heat that caused my body to burn. I was not only frightened, I was miserable.

I was in the living room that morning with my friend, who was busy braiding someone's hair. (My friend is a hair dresser.) I could tell both she and her client thought something was wrong with me by the way I acted. But neither of them said anything. I pretended I was OK, but I could not sit still. And I knew they were concerned about that.

My body felt like it was on fire—as if I were sitting on burning coals.

At the same time, I was attempting to cover my daughter with all the blankets my friend had lying on a couch in the living room. Why? I assume I was trying to comfort or protect her. As my daughter looked at me, though, she had a troubled look on her face because of all of my strange actions.

I'm sure she was wondering where the bruises on my face had come from and what had left a puffy lump under one of my eyes. But she didn't ask. And at the time, I wasn't even aware of them because I had not yet looked in a mirror.

From time to time I glanced at my friend and the woman who was having her hair braided and could see a look of suspicion on their faces. But what could I have said to calm their concerns? How could I explain a mystery that I didn't even fully understand? So I said nothing.

I then became eager for us to leave. I sort of brushed everything off and told my friend that my daughter and I were going to leave. We grabbed our things, but when I reached into the backpack, I could not find my keys. We looked everywhere in her home with no success. So I finally called for another friend's help, and her husband gave us a ride.

I left my car parked on the street at my friend's place for days. Later, after the events I'm telling you about, I had another key made for my car at the cost of nearly six hundred dollars. (It was a Benz 450—expensive to maintain.)

Now, hold that thought as I jump forward in time before continuing my story of those seven days.

A few weeks had gone by since losing my keys, when I received a call from my sister-friend one morning with news that my friend's fiancé had sent her several pictures of my key that he had found tucked into an almost full jar of *Vaseline.* The key had been hidden in the *Vaseline* jar and tucked away behind a computer. Of course they couldn't keep from wondering if I had done that. As far as they knew, no else could have. (And looking back now, I have to say it is quite possible.)

My friend's fiancé asked her if I had seen a psychiatrist. He actually saw me in my low emotional state at the time and told one of our mutual friends that I needed psychiatric help. So finding the key surely seemed to reinforce his feeling.

While others who knew me were tiptoeing around me with their true feelings about my state of mind during that whole ordeal, he was actually stating what all of them thought of me at the time but could not say to me.

Now to continue the story of my seven day journey:

I also had a Toyota automobile, and I then turned to it for transportation. Then a desire overwhelmed me to throw away things we owned. And that desire was so strong in my mind that I couldn't escape it. So driven with that desire, I emptied our whole house and gave most of our things to a thrift store while distributing the rest to various other places.

I donated all of my daughter's clothes to a children's organization and half of mine to different organizations that serve women. I had six containers full of various kinds of business clothes that I intended to donate to an organization that aids women in dressing for success for career opportunity. Unfortunately, that organization was not accepting donations due the Covid-19 pandemic. But I was able to donate those clothes to another organization.

My mind convinced me that I should not want anything I owned. I began to feel that we needed to disconnect from everything we had known—including people. So I took my phone and deleted the numbers of people who were close to me and who had been our support. I then deleted all of the social media apps and turned off my location. I followed by buying two new phones for my daughter and me and changing our phone numbers.

Oh, the consequences of the lack of spiritual enlightenment! Or perhaps I should say, "Oh, "the depth of spiritual wickedness!" For it was clearly spiritual wickedness, powers of this world's darkness, and forces of evil that I was battling and that were attempting to pull me and my daughter away from the arms of God, who clearly still loved me throughout my ordeal.

Lost and confused, I began to quote a saying of one of the preachers I had been listening to before the beginning of our seven day ordeal. He often said, "Life is spiritual." At the time, I honestly didn't get the full concept behind what he said, but even in my pathetic mental state I was beginning to understand it better.

> For we wrestle not against flesh and blood, but against principalities, against powers, against the rulers of the darkness of this world, against spiritual wickedness in high places.
>
> (Ephesians 6:12 KJV)

In my state of desperation, I then reached out again to the lead pastor and two of his associate pastors who had worked with us at the non-denominational church. We were in dire need. And at the time I knew of no one else with such a background who could help us. Everything about spiritual warfare and the reality of spiritual principalities and powers was something very new to my daughter and me.

I concluded that perhaps I had been disobedient for distancing myself from under the church's covering and for refusing to see another pastor as the lead pastor had recommended. And I rationalized that maybe I should fully try to understand more of the *gifts* I had received before relying on my own suspicions alone. Therefore, in great anguish, and with my daughter next to me looking very sick, I typed a message out on my phone and sent it to the lead pastor.

The message read as a plea for him to consider helping us. Also, I asked him if we could stay with him and his family and offered to pay rent to be under a spiritual covering. His response was, "My house would not be conducive to host you." Instead, he suggested he would, however, find us another place to stay.

I was put out by him suggesting the resolution of my situation included having me rent a room from a stranger. So I declined his offer.

Then I sent a message to the pastor who had revealed to me details about my family and my childhood, and I asked the same of him. His response was, "My home is overcrowded."

I then asked if my daughter and I could to stay in his church and spend the night there? I didn't get a response to my message. I then called him and asked if he could send someone from his church or his home to stay with my daughter and me at our place? (I considered that would perhaps work if we were not home by ourselves.) His response was, "Let me call you back."

Well, almost a year later, I am still waiting for him to call me back.

Finally, after that failed attempt I sent a message to the associate pastor who had participated in the night prayer vigils with me, and I asked him if my daughter and I could stay with him and his family. His response was "Yes."

He sent a text message to me with an address that I believed to be his home address. I was relieved. By then it was very late at night, and we had been driving all day. We were an hour away from the place where he asked us to meet him, but we went there anyway. To make that night's experience even worse, we got lost many times while trying to find the address because I was unfamiliar with the area.

We finally found the place, though, but when we arrived we found it was a run-down motel. When we arrived, my daughter and I looked at each other in disbelief. I asked her to stay in the car while I got out to meet with the associate pastor, who was there waiting in his car.

After greeting me, he immediately said, "Our home is crowded, but this is what my wife and I can do for you."

I looked him straight in the eyes and told him that my daughter and I had attempted to stay in two different hotels, but each time we tried, we met with terrible experiences of something or someone following us.

I then said, "My message to you stated that we needed to be under the covering of a man of God." I further told him I could afford to get a place of my own to stay. I wasn't seeking funding. I was seeking a spiritual place of safety, not simply a place for my daughter and me to lay our heads.

I could not help but keep my gaze on the associate pastor's face, whose own gaze was clearly focused on the bruises on my face and my overall appearance. (I had also lost a lot of weight.)

Then, even though I told him we didn't need financial help, he reached for his wallet in an attempt to give me some money. He said, "Here, take this little bit to help you out." And he continued, "All you are going through is for Kingdom work."

And yet again I corrected him. "I didn't come to you for money." And at that, I said my goodbye and walked off leaving him standing with his money and wallet in his hand.

Left with no other option, I called some friends we knew from the Catholic church and asked them to host us for the night. It was past midnight by that time. Oh, how I wish I could tell you that our experience was better at that home. But it wasn't.

I could not lie to that couple. I shared a bit about what was going on and told them I was concerned for my daughter. The husband's response was a bit comical. He said, "I hope whatever it is does not come into our home."

His concern was valid in a way. But I had come to understand that spiritual things don't work that way. It was about me and mine.

I responded and told him no, it would not. His wife's eyes were fixed on my face, so I tried to joke about my condition and told her a man did not hit me, and I was not in an abusive relationship. Neither of them laughed at that.

They were pleasant hosts, though. They allowed us to stay with them, and both husband and wife showed a level of concern and kindness for my daughter. Not long after we arrived, we said our goodnights, and we headed to the room where they lodged us.

Just as it had been a night of horror at my sister-friend's place, and a night of mystery at my other friend's place, so it was in that home. I could not close my eyes there all night—not even for a second. Only God knows what I was fighting all that night. But whatever it was, it seemed to then want to hurt my daughter.

I saw things that caused me to move from place to place in the room and in the small bathroom in the hallway next to the room. My whole body was burning, and then I began to hear the ticking sound again. I made sure my daughter was covered up entirely to the point that I thought I could suffocate her by doing more.

The wife had given me holy water before we went into the bedroom. I was moved to not use it and put it behind a dresser in the room . But I used the anointing oil that had long before become our constant companion to anoint our bodies. But then I anointed the entire room to excess, hoping to stop all that was making me uncomfortable.

Then, because of the level of fear that gripped me and the strange things I was doing in the room, I felt we could no longer stay there. So I dragged my daughter out of bed to one area of the living room and asked her to lie on the couch, where I made sure I thoroughly covered her up. And it was after that when I began to see what by that time had become a familiar pattern of snakes forming on the area rug the couple had in the center of the living room.

My daughter, being weak from not feeling well, not eating well, and not sleeping well in days, was again dragged to another side of the house by me in my attempts to shield her from danger. That kind of activity, or behavior, continued throughout the night—with us going from room to room—until it was around 6:00 AM.

It was then when I decided my daughter and I should leave—but not before I ensured the room was wiped down to clean up the anointing oil. Then I walked halfway up the stairs and called out to my friends to say we were leaving. In parting, the wife, whom by the look on her face seemed to have been a witness to the activities of our night, said to me, "I pray everything works out for you and your daughter."

In front of their home, I became very disoriented and confused—worse than ever. I could barely articulate a thing. It was as if my mind had finally left me for good.

It happened that my second car had seemed to me to become electrically charged every time I touched it, so a friend had allowed us to switch cars with him. I had not driven his car before that, so I was not sure about all its features. But I was sure that I locked the car when we arrived the night before. However, when I approached the car that morning I saw the doors were unlocked, and there was a twenty-dollar bill resting between the gearshift and the console.

I did not remember leaving money out in the open. So before starting the car and driving off, I took the twenty-dollar bill and laid it outside on the ground next to the car. I then left some of our belongings next to it and drove off.

But as we made our way out of the subdivision, I rationalized that the couple would indeed conclude that I had lost my mind if they saw the money and belongings, so I turned around to retrieve them. But that also became a difficult and bizarre effort.

I found myself driving around in the subdivision for about an hour trying to find a home I had just driven away from. I could not seem to process my surroundings. But somehow I finally managed to find the house and retrieve the items from the ground. By then it was daylight. And I'm sure either my friends or their neighbors saw me as I acted like a thief scavenging in their neighborhood.

Our first stop after leaving my friends' subdivision was a gas station nearby where I left the twenty-dollar bill in the bathroom stall. I was convinced it had been placed in the car to track us (which, I know, is crazy). Also, I left several of our items as well, which is something I started doing during those seven days in my attempt to make the culprit following us believe we were still in the area.

My daughter and I sat in the parking lot at the gas station as I contemplated where we would head next. But I had no clue. In my mind, every element of nature was against me. And it seemed the sun and moon in particular were against me. So nowhere I could drive seemed like a good place to go.

But I managed to leave the city where we were and headed to another town. There, we ended up at another gas station. Camilla and I went into the restroom, and once inside, my mind told me I should wash my hair in the sink. And I did. I removed my bandana and placed my head under the faucet. I used paper towels to dry my head.

The sun was shining as bright as it can be when we came out of the gas station. My mind then convinced me that I should dance around my car right there in the parking lot. And I did.

I danced in a circular motion while starring at the sun. I danced for several minutes as people at the gas station watched me with a puzzled look on their faces. But I was not the least bothered by their gaze, because nothing seemed abnormal to me about it.

It was as if we were living in two different worlds.

I had also washed my bandana when I washed my hair, and my mind told me to place it on the grassy area by the loading dock behind the gas station, which I did. Then I began to dance again as if I were circling the sun. All the while, the spectators continued to watch along with my daughter, who was sitting in the passenger side of the car.

I'm sure she was plenty embarrassed. But to me, I was perfectly aligned with my senses. And it turned out that dancing episode would not be the only additional strange behavior to come out of my already compromised mind.

I could hardly pray during those seven days since we were always on the go. My prayer partners—the pastor who is out of the country and his sister—were making frantic attempts to reach me to pray, but I ignored many of their attempts. My mind told me that was the right thing to do. I treated calls from my sister-friend and others the same way. But from time to time, though, I answered their calls.

On one particular call I was excited to share with my prayer partners all that was going on with me since receiving my "spiritual gifts." I remember that both of them were quiet on the other side of the line. And with that, I concluded they weren't convinced of my mental wellness but were trying to be gentle in the way they talked with me.

After praying together, they shared that they were concerned for my daughter. I assured them we were both fine. There was nothing about my intellect that allowed me to perceive I was being driven into a dark world of insanity. After all, I had previously been told by those other pastors that my behavior was normal, and it was all for the kingdom of God.

In one conversation I had with another pastor who hadn't worked on our deliverance, I shared with him about my experiences with spiritual gifts, and he even likened my behavior to that of Elijah to draw the point home to me that what I was experiencing was in fact the operation of the Holy Spirit.

So as my actions continued to reflect bizarre behavior during my seven day journey, I remained confused and completely lacked the spiritual maturity to discern what was from the Holy Spirit and what was not.

And I hate to admit the next incident, but I believe it's necessary for me to be completely transparent as I relate my journey to you. One day after using the restroom at another gas station, my mind convinced me that I should exit the restroom stall by crawling under the door instead of opening the door. And I did exactly that.

Unbeknownst to me, someone else in the restroom saw what I did and reported me to the gas station staff. One of the staff members approached my daughter due to concerns for my mental state and asked if she needed help. The staff member actually asked Camilla if they should call 911. My daughter came to me and told me about it. Then I panicked and told her we had to leave immediately. And we left quickly—but not before leaving some of our items in the one corner of the entrance doors.

You may think by now that I was becoming a spiritual lunatic during my seven day road trip, and I can't blame you for thinking that way. But my behavior got even worse before it got better.

That gas station was on a very busy road. I stopped at the gas station only to use the restroom, so I had parked my friend's car at a distance—on the other side of the road—and walked to the gas station. After parking the car, my mind had instructed me to bury the car's key in the ground for safekeeping.

That sure sounds crazy, but what's more, rather than walking back and immediately going to the car, my mind told me to sit on the ground in the middle of the busy road, which I did. I sat there in the roadway while fumbling through the few personal items we still had and threw them all away.

Only a crazy lady would do something like that, right? I understand.

So much more happened during those seven days that if I were to detail it all in this book, it could end up being the size of Tolstoy's *War and Peace*. So I won't tell of many more crazy incidents but will let you know that as the days progressed toward the end of that period things just went from bad to worse.

When I look back at all that happened to me since the beginning of 2019, I ask myself what I could have done differently to keep from having to experience so many very real days of *unreality*.

I did what seemed right to me by talking with the pastors and not hiding anything from them. And my heart was open to receive guidance from those men of God. But things had just not worked out well for me when it came to their counsel and the way they encouraged me to accept and use spiritual gifts.

Before you judge me for questioning such things let's accept what the Bible says about being under the authority of Christian leaders and minding the things of the Holy Spirit.

The writer of Hebrews said, *"Obey your leaders and submit to them, for they are keeping watch over your souls, as those who will have to give an account"* (Hebrews 13:17a ESV).[14]

Take note that in merely this one verse of the Bible we see that, yes, we are all to take seriously our responsibilities to honor the decisions and admonitions of church leaders. But we also see that those same leaders are not without their own responsibilities to God to know when and how they are to represent God when it comes to those decisions and admonitions.

Also, the Apostle John said, *"Dear friends, do not believe every spirit, but test the spirits to see whether they are from God, because many false prophets have gone out into the world"* (1 John 4:1).

John knew that not every person who says, "Thus sayeth the Lord," actually speaks for God. And he knew we should not accept all spiritual manifestations, prophecies, or teachings as having been birthed by the Holy Spirit just because that's the way they are represented.

---

14 From The Holy Bible, English Standard Version. ESV® Text Edition: 2016. Copyright © 2001 by Crossway Bibles, a publishing ministry of Good News Publishers. All rights reserved.

But even further, when writing to the Corinthian Christians to address their confusion and unruly behavior when it came to how they accepted and used spiritual gifts, Paul wrote:

For the spirits of prophets are subject to the prophets [the prophecy is under the speaker's control, and he can stop speaking]; for God [who is the source of their prophesying] is not a God of confusion and disorder but of peace and order.

(1 Corinthians 14:32-33a AMP)

I have learned through my experiences, and more importantly by studying the Bible for myself, that while we honor and follow leaders whom God has appointed over us, we not only have the right but also the responsibility to know if what they say and prophesy is in line with Scripture.

And I have learned that just as there is a time to speak out for God, there is also a time to keep it to ourselves. And if we have a responsibility to judge what others say, we also have a responsibility to judge what we say before we open our mouths.

So, yes, I began questioning the direction I received from others. But I also began questioning more and more my own involvement and responsibilities for what was happening to me.

One of the last strange incidents that happened right before my seven day journey ended happened at a city where I had worked several years earlier. My mind led me to a parking lot and directed me to open the car door and place either my right or left hand on the ground as if I were leaving a handprint on the surface of the pavement—sort of like what they do on the *Hollywood Walk of Fame.*

Then I was led to another location not too far from where I had supposedly left my handprint. And there, my mind instructed me to dance around a tree. As I danced, I began to spin around—feeling like something floating in the air. After that, I drove off yet again to another destination and continued to exhibit the same abnormal behavior here and there until it was late at night.

Oh boy!

We ended up that night staying at someone's place where my nightly experience was similar to those I have already shared with you. In the morning, however, something amazing happened. Suddenly everything seemed peaceful without any concerns on my part that I was operating abnormally. It was as if a transformation had occurred during the night that altered my state of mind. And I can't fully explain it.

As I write this, I now say with confidence that I am convinced it was only the Sovereign Hand of God that could have intervened overnight in my life. I believe He personally joined the battle that was being fought for my soul. For I was changed.

I received a call later that morning from my sister-friend, who had been calling me, but whose calls I had been ignoring. She had decided to purposely intervene in my situation with her husband and family, and she solicited help from a couple of our mutual friends. I was not aware of the arrangement they had put in place until my sister-friend and her family showed up where my daughter and I were staying that day.

When my sister-friend arrived and started to address my situation, I immediately became defensive and was ready to leave. But my sister-friend's mother, who was with her family, grabbed me by my right arm and began to chastise me. I became angry and attempted to walk into the garage. (I was already standing by the garage entry door).

I looked a mess. My hygiene was poor, and my appearance was like someone who had stopped caring for herself for a long time. Soon, the rest of the clan wanted to chime in, I refused to listen. I then asked my sister-friend to walk out of the house with me; I was willing to talk with her alone.

She, in turn, grabbed my daughter and followed me to her car.

It was likely Jeremiah, known as the weeping prophet, who wrote, *"It is of the LORD's mercies that we are not consumed, because his compassions fail not. They are new every morning: great is thy faithfulness"* (Lamentations 3:22-23 KJV).

Jeremiah could write that because he found those things to be true, and I indeed have also found them to be true for my daughter and me.

My sister-friend, who had bottled up a well of tears over what had been our state of being during the previous seven days—but was unprepared to confront me until that day—was by then crying uncontrollably. Then it was my daughter's turn to let out all of her emotions. For over an hour, the two of them cried as I sat next to them in the car, taking it all in.

After experiencing what a week of darkness had manifested itself in my life, I honestly don't know how I could not have cried too. But instead, I felt only a determination to spread my wings and soar into a new existence—as a butterfly must feel who remembers what it was like to be a caterpillar.

I had a conviction that the dark cloud had been removed and it was all over, which were my repeated words to my sister-friend and daughter, who were still crying. But they struggled to believe me since nothing about my physical state gave them any assurance. I understand now how difficult it must have been for them to place their trust in whatever I had to say after the way I had acted for so long.

My sister-friend began to press in with her daily account of all I had done during the seven days. She grabbed the backpack and plastic bags that were our luggage, and she grabbed my new phone that I attempted to destroy a couple of days earlier by submerging it in a bowl of hot water—because I was convinced we were being tracked through the phone (I hadn't told you about that)—and said, "None of this is you!"

Then she addressed my physical appearance. She voiced her displeasure over how I had been acting around people who had great respect for me. I mean, she really let me have it as my daughter listened in tears.

Interestingly, I then found out the things she was saying to me were things she had already been discussing in confidence with my daughter before that day in her attempt to keep Camilla calm and of sound mind. While my sister-friend was admonishing me, she turned and looked at my daughter and said, "Have I not been talking to you about this?"

Then under the same breath, with tears in her eyes, she looked at me and said, "You are not crazy, ma'am!" (We call each other Ma'am.) Continuing, she said, "This is not true, and it's not you." Then she added, "I have rejected what people around me have been trying to convince me to believe about your state of mind, and I've refused to put you on a psychiatric hold, which is what some of them are pressing me to do."

Then she begged me to return home and trust God to finish the process of restoring me. But she not only just begged me to return home but also sent her twelve-year-old son with us to stay with us for a while.

It is written in Proverbs that *a friend loves at all times, and a brother is born for adversity"* (Proverbs 17:17 AMP). Believe me, my sister-friend is a Proverbs 17:17 friend with whom my daughter and I are profoundly linked. To God be the glory!

After such a morning as that, where else could I have gone but home?

But before arriving home that afternoon, my daughter, my sister-friend's son, and I stopped to buy some food, a few household items, and air mattresses. I had given away everything we owned. A ray of sunlight was visible on my daughter's face. And I assumed she must have been thinking, "At last, this nightmare is over!"

Once we arrived home, she was herself again and enjoying being with my friend's son, who had been her best pal since they were both toddlers.

I received a call around 9:00 PM that night from the pastor of the church I had left. During the call, he assured me that the activities—or the experiences—I had during the seven days were normal, because Elijah experienced kind of the same.

Huh? Normal? I had read in the Bible about Elijah being violently opposed and succumbing to a time of depression. But I never read about Elijah seeing snakes on the floor or in the air, viewing shadowy figures following him, feeling things crawling on him, or doing anything at all like what I had been doing for seven days!

Further, I thought the pastor was calling to pray with me. But he said, "I only called to hear your voice." And without praying he said his goodbye.

Excuse me? As strange as it may sound, my experience with that call made it apparent to me that I needed to disconnect completely from all those pastors permanently. Sure, the Lord used them for my benefit in some ways, but that didn't necessarily mean they always followed after, pursued, and delivered God's truth.

Before our lives were interrupted by those events, I had put our home up for sale. I decided to sell it and use the equity I had in it to expand my private homecare business. Ironically, the average home sold in my subdivision within thirty days or less. However, our home did not sell despite us having fully renovated it both inside and out.

Considering we didn't have much money since I used my savings to renovate our home, I was nervous about my finances because I had not worked in almost a year. I knew selling our home would eliminate our financial burden. One day I was discussing my homecare business with my accountant when in the midst of our conversation she advised me to file for unemployment.

I honestly don't know why that came up since our discussion was not related to my personal financial struggles. But I know God often speaks through other people, so I followed my accountant's advice and filed for unemployment. That happened during the time when there was lots of discussion about unemployment benefits because of the impact the Covid-19 pandemic had on the economy.

The approval process was challenging for a lot of people. But God stepped in and made a way for me. And within a month of applying, I was granted approval and began receiving a weekly unemployment benefit.

But we ran out of money before I started receiving the unemployment benefits. It was as if every financial avenue had dried up. We had been at the mercy of my sister-friend and a couple of other friends who had given us some money and helped us buy some of what we needed. So receiving unemployment when I did was a blessing.

God uses people, and I rejoice in the interventions and sovereignty of Jehovah Jireh![15]

My daughter, who is very reserved, had not spoken at all about our seven days' journey. So recently, to see if she would talk to me about it, I shared with her what that hotel attendant had written in his nightly report.

Camilla then turned, looked at me, and said, "Mommy, if I didn't know you, I would have thought you were crazy." And she added, "Those days were awful, my gosh! I hope it never happens again."

I laughed! It was the hardest I had laughed in a long time, because I recognized it was only the Hand of God that brought me back from the depths of darkness. And only through His grace could I look back through all of it and laugh while giving all the credit to God for delivering me from my enemies—and even from myself.

It may cause you to wonder how one could be so far gone mentally and end up soon thereafter writing a book to encourage others who struggle with either life in general or with an enemy

15 Roughly translated into English: the Lord who provides.

who has a strong hold on their lives for whatever reason. But isn't that kind of turnaround at the core of the gospel?

Why, yes. Yes it is!

I will be your God throughout your lifetime until your hair is white with age. I made you, and I will care for you. I will carry you along and save you. (Isaiah 46:4 NLT)

CHAPTER 11

The Voice of God

After the earthquake came a fire, but the LORD was not in the fire.
And after the fire came a gentle whisper.   (1 Kings 19:12)

I BELIEVE THE above verse is strikingly appropriate when it comes to thinking about our experiences as we continued to settle in after what had been seven days of turbulence.

For whatever reason, although the great Jehovah-Raah[16] was with my daughter and me during that time, God did not speak to me in a forceful way to direct me or lead me out of trouble—or if He did, I was not able to recognize it. But after the seventh day ended, God clearly spoke to me through a gentle whisper, which brought to me a sense of calmness within.

I have come to know that God intends for His voice, regardless of how it comes to us, to shepherd us through the distractions around us in order to lead us into the place of stillness and peace,

---

16 Roughly translated to English: The Lord who Shepherds, or The Lord my Shepherd.

which is often our most desperate need.

And as far as *when* God speaks, He is famous for always being on time! In the account of Lazarus in John chapter eleven, Jesus appeared to be late to heal Lazarus. He waited four days to travel to Bethany after being told Lazarus was sick, and He did not reach the home of Lazarus, Mary, and Martha until Lazarus had died. But Jesus demonstrated God was always on time when He raised Lazarus from the dead. For that's exactly what He planned to do all along.

We became planted in the fortitude of God's canopy after our seven day ordeal. It seemed He had translated us from the dominion of darkness into His Kingdom of Light.[17] We were brought into an inheritance that was already ours, but lack of knowledge of the Word of God had hindered us from knowing it. However, God, who is always merciful, patiently waited for us—more specifically, for *me*.

Still somewhat reeling from what we had endured, I still could not fully process what the transformation I was experiencing entailed except that I knew God was taking control. So we did our best to simply accept and receive what God had delivered and was still delivering to us as we continued to pray and fast. And it seemed that the grace to pray had been given to me more than before.

God's gentle voice continued to speak to me, and I could tell many of the prayers I was praying were not of my own accord. Rather, I sensed it had to be the Spirit of Truth, the Holy Spirit, who was giving me utterance according to the will of God. And

17 "For he has rescued us from the dominion of darkness and brought us into the kingdom of the Son he loves, in whom we have redemption, the forgiveness of sins" (Colossians 1:13-14).

in time I noticed that my prayers at times almost sounded like well-written sermons of a trained preacher. They seemed directly and specifically focused on specific needs and in line with what we were facing while imploring the mercies and grace of God upon our lives.

The pastor from out of the country and his sister remained faithful to my daughter and me and continued to pray with us. We had corporate evening prayer sessions at least five days a week for about an hour and at times even longer. After the chaotic seven days were over, my continual prophesying subsided, but I had gained the grace for even more endurance to pray.

God was deep into the process of transforming my life, but don't think my battle for total freedom from the enemy and my search for spiritual maturity were over. For while the uninhibited prophesying and the over-active behavioral episodes died down, I began screaming at the top of my lungs during prayer—I mean screams like you would not believe.

I felt a huge amount of energy when praying and felt no need to hold back such emotional outbursts. But I noticed that along with the screams came a strong and toxic-smelling odor from my breath. It was as if I had swallowed a can of tear gas,[18] or as if something poisonous had been injected into my lungs.

Also, about that same time I started noticing a feeling that an area on the back of my head where I had experienced hair loss was suddenly draining down into my left ear and onto the left side of my back. And when I screamed it felt like someone

18 I am familiar with the smell and effects of tear gas because civilians living in Freetown experienced it during military conflicts when I lived there as a young person.

had shot a huge amount of jelly into the back of head that flowed into my left ear, down on the back of my left shoulder, and into my chest.

After that, it started feeling like the incision I had earlier felt being engraved on the back of my left shoulder moved around from my shoulder to under my left armpit in a wrapping motion. And it happened with such force that it caused my left breast to hurt badly. And before long, it seemed that my heart rhythm was being changed by it.

Many times during those screaming episodes I actually felt like I could be having a heart attack. And after such episodes I would become very weak and unable to do much physically. The things I'm listing here increased over time to the point that the manifestations were a daily occurrence. I mean, all it took to trigger such feelings was for me to pray or do any activities that were connected to God.

But all I knew to do was pray, so I prayed throughout the day. I had an urge to be in the presence of God continually. So I dealt with such manifestations throughout the day and during our corporate evening prayers. One day during prayer time with the pastor and his sister, I asked them about the screams, as they had not said anything about them while we were praying together. They both responded in agreement and told me the power of the Holy Spirit was working through me to eliminate everything impure that was not of God.

I wondered about what could be so impure that it would cause me to scream at such a high pitch every day. But then I reframed my thoughts and remembered those words—"life is spiritual." And at that, I could only utter, "Abba, Father, great mysteries surround your heavenlies!"

He uncovers mysteries hidden in darkness; he brings light to the
deepest gloom. (Job 12:22 NLT)

It seemed like day after day the screams and manifestations were getting louder and louder, and stranger and stranger. Then one day while praying it was if I had been thrown to the floor, and as I continued to pray I rolled from side to side on the floor as I trembled. I was alert during all those episodes. I didn't understand what all of that was about, but I was inclined on my own to believe that something was not right.

Clearly, I knew I had a questionable family background. I had messed with what I have come to understand was a wrong and spiritually dangerous way to find answers through a so-called dream interpreter. And I had allowed several pastors whose backgrounds I really knew nothing about have full control of our spiritual discipleship.

And even though I knew God was faithfully working in me in the midst of all of it, I knew there was still something very wrong! My heart told me I needed God to provide to me a final solution to my quest for complete peace in Him and freedom from the oppression of the enemy.

Left with nowhere else to turn, I continued to read my Bible faithfully and study the Word of God in addition to the many hours spent in prayer. But those were not all of the spiritual activities the Holy Spirit was training me to cultivate. I also began to listen to the recorded and published preaching and teachings of preachers and evangelists like Kenneth E. Hagin, Charles Spurgeon, Oral Roberts, Reinhard Bonnke, Kathryn Kuhlman—all of whom are now gone—and others whose teachings and preaching were of faith, salvation, and the power of the Holy Spirit.

I began to learn that the teachings and the Word of God are more simple when the one who is doing the preaching and teaching truly operates by the Spirit of God and truly knows and applies the Scripture. I concluded that although God in His grace had used people less determined to understand God's Word—and less apt to operate in the wisdom of the Holy Spirit—to start a work in me and my daughter, we had also been bamboozled in so many ways.

It was like we needed to learn many things all over to get them right.

To be clear, I also devoted time to learn from the teachings of current pastors and evangelists who are reputable in handling Scripture and following God. But something drove me to seek what so often seems to be missing in the Church today. So I found myself gravitating more toward the teachings and preaching of the men and women of old.

In them, I believe I discovered what we lacked—the missing pieces to the puzzle to connect and uncover the mysteries of our lives. My desire to learn of God and of His Word—not only as it pertained to our situation but also to my quest to know Him better—became like a sweet-smelling aroma that intoxicated me and drew me closer.

Also, the admonishments of the Apostle Peter often resonated with me.

But grow (spiritually mature) in the grace and knowledge of our Lord and Savior Jesus Christ. To Him be the glory (honor, majesty, splendor) both now and to the day of eternity. Amen.
(2 Peter 3:18 AMP)

Peter, coming full circle into his complete identity as a child of God, admonished us to desire to fully know God and his Son, Jesus, with full reverence.

I took heed to Peter's advice and continued to dig deep in my communication with God. I talked with the Lord often as I read my Bible. And as I did, I also continued to listen to what by that time had definitely become important training tools under the direction of the Holy Spirit—the preaching and teaching of respected men and women of God.

I also continued my prayer sessions with the pastor and his sister who lived outside the country. And one night during one of our corporate prayer sessions, I said to the pastor, "I don't believe those screams are from the Holy Spirit." I credit my arrival at that belief to the late Kathryn Kuhlman, whose love and defense of the Holy Spirit was unlike any I have come to know.

The pastor then responded and said, "No, it's not." He continued, "You can't ask a lot of questions when dealing with spiritual matters."

I was unsure what that statement implied, so I pressed him the following day to clarify it for me. He said, "Often, deliverance takes time, because many spiritual afflictions could result in the person dying if not handled correctly."

I didn't exactly agree with the pastor's statement, but I took it under advisement. Then I charged myself to learn all the truth behind our mystery.

I knew we belonged to God, which means our lives are His, and no one could take that from us. So trusting I would always continue to belong to God, I turned to the Scriptures to encourage my faith.

I read that *"without faith it is impossible to please God"* (Hebrews 11:6a).

Then I read about Moses leaving Egypt.

By faith he left Egypt, not fearing the king's anger; he persevered because he saw him who is invisible. (Hebrews 11:27)

I knew my faith needed to be stirred. I knew I had to relinquish all fears. And I concluded that I must leave my spiritual *Egypt* behind.

So I studied the Word of God with renewed vigor. And I continued to press into prayer. I fasted—even fasting once for a full three days without eating and drinking anything. I sowed seeds—gave offerings and tithed—which I always knew are biblical principles. And as I continued to pursue all of those activities with more determination to increase and exhibit faith, I could tell the Lord was on our side.

And I could also tell that what had invaded or attacked my body became very uncomfortable with it all.

I suffered terribly as whatever was tormenting me began to display a high level of displeasure over the enlightenment I was receiving through the Word of God. The attacks on my body became progressively worse. I was weakened and felt beaten down to the point that I could hardly eat or move. But I kept the momentum going with my prayers, because I believed prayer was the weapon that kept digging at my dark tormentor to remove it from me.

Shortly thereafter, I realized I was no longer speaking in tongues. That was the remaining "gift" I had received that I was regularly exhibiting. And frankly, I became grateful that all of the manifestations of the spirit world were out of my system. Don't misunderstand me, I do believe in the Gifts of the Holy Spirit—just as they are listed in 1 Corinthians 12:7-11.[19]

But as I was finally learning, the demonstrations of my "gifts" were not characteristic of the way the Holy Spirit—who is gentle, intelligent, and orderly—operates in the Church.

I noticed that the more I learned from Scripture, and the more the true Spirit of God worked through me, the more enlightened I became at differentiating what is and what is not of God. I became aware that just as the Holy Spirit can come to us and influence us to do things to bring Glory to God and His kingdom, so can other forces in the spirit world for the purpose of causing confusion by mimicking God's work.

So I began to make different declarations using the Word of God when I prayed. That often meant that while studying the Word, a Bible verse or chapter stood out to me, and I used it to pray and declare the truth of God.

And that seemed to finally start bringing my spiritual battle to a head.

One day as I engaged in studying God's Word and declaring its truth in prayer, I heard a voice say, "I will never let you go."

I froze dead in place and wondered, "Would the Holy Spirit say such a thing?"

19 "Now to each one the manifestation of the Spirit is given for the common good. To one there is given through the Spirit a message of wisdom, to another a message of knowledge by means of the same Spirit, to another faith by the same Spirit, to another gifts of healing by that one Spirit, to another miraculous powers, to another prophecy, to another distinguishing between spirits, to another speaking in different kinds of tongues, and to still another the interpretation of tongues. All these are the work of one and the same Spirit, and he distributes them to each one, just as he determines" (1 Corinthians 12:7-11).

I didn't know what to make of it, so I continued studying and handed it over to God. Following that, many similar interruptions occurred during my prayers while I continued to be diligent in pressing into knowing more about the Word of God. I somehow knew I was *hitting the nail on the head*, so to speak, so it started to become clear to me that the goal of my tormenter was to scare me and intimidate me into stopping.

However (and pardon my use of words here—but they are intentional), there was no chance encounter in hell that I was going to stop the pace at which I was then operating in my determination to gain that which our Lord Jesus had won for us on Calvary—**Freedom**.

I knew I and my family had to break free of what had influenced and in large part controlled our spiritual lives for so long. It was something that could not remain in or around us.

I then received further encouragement from the Word to persevere in my battle against the enemy.

Are not two little sparrows sold for a copper coin? And yet not one of them falls to the ground apart from your Father's will. But even the very hairs of your head are all numbered [for the Father is sovereign and has complete knowledge]. So do not fear; you are more valuable than many sparrows. (Matthew 10:29-31 AMP)

I consumed those words of Jesus recorded by Matthew and rejoiced that God himself had ultimate control over our lives. I determined once again to fulfill my responsibility to trust God and have faith in Him.

I became aware that I was able to better discern some spiritual things. But I didn't have anyone to talk to at the time about what was happening to me. Various spiritual manifestations were still taking place, and one of them caused my right hand to shake violently one day.

Additionally, as I read the Bible, I started verbally speaking things out loud about what God was preparing me for. Many of those statements that appeared to me as words of wisdom, which is what the Bible speaks about, seemed genuine. But I didn't take them at face value—especially since they ended up coming to me on a daily basis as I read the Bible. So as they came to me I began recording them by writing them down in my Bible on the pages I was reading at the time and dated them accordingly.

Then, as I knelt to pray with Camilla one night, a crawling sensation on my left shoulder intensified like someone was again carving something on my shoulder blade. I screamed and fell to the floor. Then I heard a voice say to me, "Be strong." He continued—yes, *he*; it was the voice of a man—"I am preparing you for greatness."

Was I hearing from God, or not? Believe me, I felt like nothing I had been reading or studying in the Bible all during my lengthy involvements with spiritual manifestations—or even over my entire life—compared to what I was experiencing. We clearly needed more of God, so I prayed earnestly for His help.

As I continued to seek God, my mind prompted me to register for graduate school (which had been my desire before everything started to happen). Within a week, I had applied and gained admission to one of the prestigious universities in Atlanta, Georgia.

After having a consultation with the admissions director, he advised me that the masters of divinity program would best fit what I was aiming to do with my degree. I started graduate school, hoping to graduate within two years and launch into ministry. God is truly merciful! Because within a week I realized I was dealing with another attempt of the enemy to keep me from what God had orchestrated for my life as a part of *His* action plan.

I did not pray one time during the first week of classes. In fact, I was overwhelmed with my classes to the point that I had no time to engage in any of my spiritual activities, and the attacks of the enemy were not subsiding. I remember being on a web conference as I participated in a class one day. I looked at myself on the screen and realized I appeared so disheveled and lost that I began to question if that speedy admission to a prominent university was actually a gift from God or something else.

I soon withdrew from graduate school to keep it from appearing negatively on my transcript. But that did not cause me to question my calling into the ministry even if I considered that I likely got ahead of God's plan for me. So in that, I knew I had no doubt once again thwarted the enemy's plans, because my discouragement over my decision to attend graduate school did not affect my resolve to find the path God wanted me to take. The enemy was not happy, and I didn't care.

I knew I was still learning to hear God's voice.

Following my experience with the graduate school I became focused on going to war with the forces that ran amuck in my family. I confessed before all the enemies of God that whatever agreement was made by anyone in the past, it was not my doing. I never vowed to worship anything other than God.

I admitted what God knows very well; I am not perfect. I have committed my share of sins. But I never in any way knowingly violated the sacred covenant of serving only God by seeking or accepting an occult, idolatrous, or devilish path. I may not have always made the best decisions in life, but I have always known that my daughter and I belong to the family of heaven.

I determined and took a stand that our lives were not up for grabs.

I was bold in my views and stood against the enemy, but I must caution you, brethren, such audacity to challenge the enemy is developed only with an awareness of one's position in God.

Prophesying to Daniel of the actions of the "king of the north," the messenger God sent to Daniel (likely a high-ranking angel) said, *"He will flatter and win over those who have violated the covenant. But the people who know their God will be strong and will resist him"* (Daniel 11:32 NLT).

Note that the people who will be strong and resist the enemy are those who know their God and do not violate His covenant. Resisting temptations and assaults with the Word of God and the power of the Holy Spirit guarantees us the victory in any battle. Nevertheless, one must be born again and truly know and follow God to boldly and confidently confront the enemy.

Fully immersed in my study of the Word and absorbing all I could learn as I was being taught by the Holy Spirit, I sensed I was also becoming restless—mainly because of how I felt physically and mentally. I began to feel angry. I continued to remember and have mixed emotions over how our matter was handled by those whom I trusted to help me, which I deemed to be a failure.

Then my mind started shifting wildly from one thing to another. I even started to rationalize and think that perhaps if my mother would die, maybe, just maybe, everything would cease and the battle would be over. After all, as the pastors said, she is the "point of contact" with the enemy, and her own actions when she stayed with us did not leave me with anything to make me believe otherwise.

But I came to realize that my anger and such thoughts about my mother's faults were simply being used by the enemy to lure me once again into his trap. So I shifted my focus back to simply trusting God by casting all of my emotions on Him. I concluded that if I continued to dwell on my feelings, they would only stand in the way of me finding God's final solution to my problems.

I found true encouragement to do that in words written in Isaiah.

All who rage against you will be ashamed and disgraced. All who contend with you will perish and disappear. You will look for your enemies in vain; those who war against you will vanish without a trace! I am Yahweh, your mighty God! I grip your right hand and won't let you go! I whisper to you: "Don't be afraid; I am here to help you!" (Isaiah 41:11-13 TPT)

And these words were enough to empower me to reposition myself in Him!

———

I was getting stronger in both my spirit and my confidence in my Lord, and soon that set the stage for me to conclude that if we have the victory in our spiritual battle, we most certainly can have it in our finances.

Of course, my finances did not exactly testify to that, for there was no movement on the sale of our house. And both of my businesses were at a standstill. I was unable to work because of my health. But after months of praying, fasting, and seeking God's intervention for a financial breakthrough, appointments for house showings began to come in.

We had several showings, but none of them turned into offers. The process was hard on both my daughter and me because we had to leave our house every time a request came in to show the home. Rain or shine, each time there was a showing, we left and went and stayed at our neighborhood's clubhouse, and sometimes we would stay there for hours.

It was taking a significant toll on Camilla because she was in school, and many of the showings were during school hours. (This was during the Covid-19 pandemic, and she was doing remote schooling at home.)

I remember on several occasions as we walked to the clubhouse to wait during a showing, I prayed a simple prayer: "Lord, have mercy for her sake!" I continued to encourage my daughter that God would come through for us. I made it a point to stir her faith in God daily and assure her that God would always grant her the victory no matter what things looked like. Instilling a strong and vibrant faith in my daughter was crucial to me.

Then yet another appointment for a showing was confirmed, and once again we walked to the clubhouse. After the showing, we came home and waited for a follow-up call, but nothing came. It was common for me to send a text message to the agents after a showing to request feedback. But that day it somehow slipped my mind (or God orchestrated it that way), and I didn't follow up with the agent.

Then around 10:00 PM that night, I decided to check my email. As I did, I saw in bold letters the subject line on a new message that read,

"YOUR HOUSE!"

I jumped from the air mattress and called for my daughter to read the email with me. The showing was a success! The buyer wanted our home.

God had spoken to us in both loud voices and still small voices. And I was learning to differentiate God's voice from others. Regardless of how I heard His voice, though, I was learning most of all that it could be trusted. And through the sale of the house, I also understood more about how He wanted to speak to us through our circumstances.

It was the voice of God speaking to us even then to let us know we could trust Him to meet all of our needs *according to the riches of his glory in Christ Jesus.*" [20]

Understanding our position, I knew I needed to be diligent. We were in a spiritual battle, and the enemy, my adversary, was out to get me. So on several occasions, I asked my prayer partners and sister-friend to do a corporate fast for several days with my daughter and me.

In the book of Zephaniah, we read:

> *Then I will give to the peoples [clear and pure speech from] purified lips [which reflect their purified hearts], that all of them may call on the name of the LORD, to serve Him shoulder to shoulder (united).*　　　　(Zephaniah 3:9 AMP)

---

20 Philippians 4:19.

We needed God's grace, and having the support of the family of believers God had given to us was vital. We learned who we could depend on. And they are still the ones who will stand shoulder to shoulder with us in time of hardship and battle.

If you have encountered any spiritual battle of any kind, you will likely agree with me that sometimes the more you pray and engage in the things of God, the more difficult things can become—and the more you need others. Well, it was no different in our case.

I applied every spiritual principle I had learned during that time while enlisting the help of fellow believers I could trust. And they also were being used by God to help me recognize, hear, and be guided by God's voice.

But nothing was happening fast enough for me, of course. While making progress in many ways, I was still suffering in other ways, and it was as if God was testing my aptitude for patience to see how faithful I would be to fully trust His care and sovereignty.

But I stayed planted in the Word of God and never took my eyes off of the Master. Rather, I pressed further into trusting Him with determination.

And one thing for sure, while I developed a better understanding of God's voice and how to separate His voice from others, I continued to learn I could depend on the way He spoke through Scripture. Undoubtedly, God had already, for many years, been communicating to me in a way that continued to point me to His Word (even if I didn't always understand what He was doing—or even saying sometimes).

And as time passed—even when I was not patient—He continued carrying out His plan to transform my life. And bit by bit, I was learning that He was not just speaking to me; He was personally teaching me and showing me the way I should go.

> This is what the LORD says—
> your Redeemer, the Holy One of Israel:
> "I am the LORD your God,
>   who teaches you what is best for you,
>   who directs you in the way you should go."
>
> (Isaiah 48:17)

CHAPTER 12

Exposing the Enemy

God [approaching from Sinai] comes from Teman (Edom), and the Holy One from Mount Paran. Selah (pause and calmly think of that). His splendor and majesty covers the heavens. And the earth is full of His praise. His brightness is like the sunlight; He has [bright] rays flashing from His hand, and there [in the sunlike splendor] is the hiding place of His power.

(Habakkuk 3:3-4 AMP)

THE LORD HAD been merciful and allowed our home to sell. We began looking for a new place and found an apartment in a complex we liked. I allowed my daughter to select it because I could tell she was a bit sad. She had lived in our previous home since kindergarten.

A day before the scheduled closing on the sale of our house, we were assured by the apartment complex management that we could take possession of the apartment at noon the following day—the day of closing on our house's sale. Camilla and I were not expecting any delays (or any mysterious interventions that only God could orchestrate).

But there were delays—with the apartment complex staff not getting things in order. I mean it was setback after setback. We were not given an exact new time for taking possession of the apartment, but we were told we could possibly begin moving in around 3:00 PM. Nevertheless, we ended up going to closing later that afternoon without knowing when we could move into our apartment.

Finally, though, late that afternoon while we were still at closing, I received an email notice that our apartment was ready for us. So immediately after closing we raced to what we presumed would become our new home.

Immediately upon arriving there, though, it seemed something was wrong by the way the staff member who met us there acted. As quickly as my thoughts began racing through my mind, the person asked, "Do you have your insurance and the information from the light company?"

I responded and said I did not due to the many back and forth delays that had taken place. At that, she took us to do the walkthrough. Then, during the walkthrough, she said, "I cannot grant you access unless you have the lights in your name and the rental's insurance."

I looked at the time. It was almost 6:00 PM. I was confused, and she was unmoved. She stood there with a stern look on her face staring at me with her eyes opened wide with an evil look to them. I thought of my daughter, who was standing beside me with a look of disbelief.

There was no negotiating with her. I got on my phone and called to have the electricity account put in my name. And I was successful. However, I couldn't get the insurance, so I asked the woman if she would allow me to get the insurance first thing in the morning. She refused.

At that, I became visibly upset, and I pointed out to her how their many delays had cost me money. I had to put my entire office in a storage unit earlier in the day, and I suffered other expenses due to their failures. But telling her about that got me nowhere.

Finally realizing she was not going to change her mind, my daughter and I left. The woman had become someone completely different from the person with whom I had been communicating for weeks and right up to just a few minutes prior to walking the unit.

As we were leaving, I called my sister-friend, and she could tell I was upset as I related to her what had taken place. Her response was, "Do not push to stay there. It's not where you need to be." I recognized she was not speaking from her own intellect but by the counsel of the Holy Spirit, but I sobbed like a baby as we drove away.

As was the case many times during the time of my afflictions, my daughter proved to be the stronger person and simply said, "Let's go to a hotel."

I allowed Camilla to choose the hotel, which she did. And it turned out that we stayed there for seven days. I thought, "Well, the Lord had the Israelites dwell in temporary shelters for seven days as part of a memorial that would point to His sovereignty during their exodus from Egypt."[21]

While at the hotel I had time to reflect on what our lives had become since the later part of 2018. I also began to ponder other details from my life that my mind was rebirthing. I even began to process more childhood memories.

As a toddler, I fell from a two or three story building. I went between the bars on a handrail and dropped to land on a concrete surface. But as explained by my mother, I was unhurt without having even a scratch on my body.

I also remembered that as a child and through my teenage years, I could not talk because I had a stuttering problem so severe that my right hand would beat against my leg as I attempted to form my words.

And then my mind shifted to the things that I had learned only recently when my mother was put in a situation by the pastor to have to address her past actions.

I then started remembering the many earaches I had since childhood, particularly in my left ear. And I remembered how it always felt like something heavy was in it. I could always tell that I could hear better with my right ear than my left. As an adult I sought medical help for it on several occasions. But all the tests continually came back showing no problem, so I learned to manage it.

Then I thought, "What's the relationship between my childhood—when people referred to me as not being 'an ordinary child'—to my current life as an adult?"

---

21 "Live in temporary shelters for seven days: All native-born Israelites are to live in such shelters so your descendants will know that I had the Israelites live in temporary shelters when I brought them out of Egypt. I am the LORD your God" (Leviticus 23:42-43).

It dawned on me that, regardless of any relationship of my present to the past, the devil knew all along what I represented on this earth. And although he is not all-knowing, like God, the enemy must have known something or assumed something about God's plan for my life. So he had tried with many attempts to stop me since I was a babe.

But if God is in a thing, it is futile to try to thwart His plan. When in their fury and hatred the members of the Sanhedrin were planning to kill Peter and the other apostles, one of them, Gamaliel, stood up and told them:

> *Men of Israel, consider carefully what you intend to do to these men. . . . Leave these men alone! Let them go! For if their purpose or activity is of human origin, it will fail. But if it is from God, you will not be able to stop these men; you will only find yourselves fighting against God.* (Acts 5:35-39)

The devil, and all enemies of the Cross, will ultimately fail to thwart God's plans, but they will never stop trying. And that means they will never stop trying to stop what God intends to do in and through both your life and mine.

I maintained the same schedule for our devotions while at the hotel, but I decided to set specific days for us to fast. Many of the sensations I experienced in my body were still present. Nothing seemed different in that regard except that we were no longer at home. We had believed God for a change in those things and assumed that was the time when we would begin to experience such change. But we needed more patience

Jesus said, *"Therefore I tell you, whatever you ask for in prayer, believe that you have received it, and it will be yours"* (Mark 11:24).

But not being fully trained, I was looking to see results with my natural eyes, which actually negates how things operate in the spiritual realm. I couldn't grasp how I could possess something before I first saw it in my possession or held it in my hand.

But I know now what the writer of Hebrews was talking about when he wrote, *"Now faith is the substance of things hoped for, the evidence of things not seen"* (Hebrews 11:1 KJV).

So I didn't need to worry about seeing (which as I said was my natural response); I simply needed to enter a new realm of trust (which is what I was beginning to do). In the process, I began to learn that *Believing Faith* is a gift from God, and one cannot obtain it by merely speaking and seeing. Action is vitally important.

I learned that I needed to make sure all of my actions stood on the foundation of faith. In other words, just as a building's foundation gives the building stability and allows its walls to stand strong against the elements that could otherwise overcome and destroy it, the foundation of faith will stabilize, secure, and strengthen my actions.

I tell you, when you position yourself to receive help from God, it's assuring to know you will receive that help.

In His delivery of the Beatitudes during His sermon on the mount, Jesus said, *"Blessed are those who hunger and thirst for righteousness, for they shall be filled"* (Matthew 5:6 NKJV). My confidence that God would supply the things I desired was growing stronger because I knew I was making my *hunger and thirst for righteousness* my first priority as I continued to patiently pursue God's will for us and learn more about faith.

As I continued to pray during those days, the energy I had to spend much time in prayer and worship could not have come from my own strength. I mentioned that I had been fasting, and the physical level at which I was able to operate was clearly supernatural.

Everything seemed different in every way. And when I read the Bible, I realized a level of understanding came to me that I did not have before. It is as if God had given me a spiritual lens to look through.

I felt empowered!

We were finally able to get a place. It was in a different town from where we wanted to be, but at least we had a place of our own to stay. There at our new place, God continued to work in my life to expose the enemy and deliver me from my oppressors **His way**.

One day while studying the Word and worshiping, I heard a voice say, "Shut up!" And those words were repeated over and over again in an agitated and aggressive tone.

I was not as puzzled as I had been the first time I heard such a voice speak. I thought, "Here comes my answer to what the Holy Spirit has been silently whispering in my spirit for so long—'Something is out of place.'"

I didn't know whether I should respond to the voice or not, so I did nothing about it. Instead, I simply continued with my devotions. But it turned out that experience soon progressed into something more.

One day I was reading about the prophet Jeremiah when, suddenly, my whole body shook in nervousness. Then without even considering to do such a thing, my right hand was moved to slap me twice on my right cheek. Wait, that was not all! I also slapped my forehead and heard that voice once again issue the command to shut up!

That probably would have scared to death most people, and some of them might have considered calling a psychiatrist. But of course odd spiritual attacks on my person that either felt real or actually were indeed physically real had become somewhat commonplace.

I knew I was in the middle of a real, genuine, knock-down-drag-out spiritual battle, so I determined once again to not yield but instead continue my devotions.

But I soon found out that day had only set a preliminary course for what was to come.

The Holy Spirit had finally exposed what I had suspected all along—that part of the experiences in my physical body and prophecies were not what others had believed them to be.

During prayer one day, I found myself speaking these words: "Every time you speak, you pierce my heart."

I will not tire from emphasizing to you the importance of studying God's Word and being in His presence in prayer and worship. It will save your life! While other spiritual exercises are essential, I found that revelations of what was actually happening in the spirit world began to be revealed to me at a greater measure the more God allowed me the ability to read my Bible, pray, worship, and fast.

I could write a thousand-page book about my and my daughter's experiences with the enemy. But my goal is not to write a lengthy book that sheds light on the activities of darkness. So believe it or not, I am sharing only some of the incidents to hopefully help you understand that God is bigger and greater than anything the enemy would dare attempt to put you through.

I made a mental note of what that voice said to me over time as I continued to hear it. I felt I needed to know more about it and needed God to show me what to do, because I didn't have any reference to help me understand it, nor had I experienced such a thing before.

I developed a mid-morning schedule to sit in my office, read my Bible, and commune with God. In so doing, I asked again and again for the Holy Spirit to help me with specific prayer points. Ever faithful, He did. And through that, I gained a level of boldness that came upon me and made it apparent to me there was no room for fear.

I was astonished at what was taking place. I admitted to being a baby Christian, but partnered with the Spirit of God, I felt I was becoming a force to be reckoned with. The intruder was not pleased, and my body again suffered the consequences of my tormenter's wrath. But something stranger began to happen as I prayed specific prayers directly relating to what was by that time recognized by me to be something foul.

It began to cry out through me as if the heat was too much to take as the Power of God worked in me. That voice ended up saying things like, "Please, Jesus help me." "I am leaving now." "I am going away today." "I was supposed to kill you, but I can't because you are God's child."

As I found myself saying those and similar words, my entire body was doing its own thing. I was manifesting things like you wouldn't believe. Then at times the enemy began to insult me with derogatory outbursts, such as, "You stupid B . . .." or, "You are a dumb B . . .." And there were other vile, insulting words—I mean wild and crazy curse words.

Then I began to scream again. But that time the screams were even louder than before. And with the screams came the feeling that someone had placed a bowl of jelly-like substance inside the right side of my face. And the louder I screamed the more I felt like the jelly-like substance was draining through my nose and into my throat and chest. Then, I had a crawling sensation on the top of my head as if something was fighting to move or make its exit.

As all that was happening, I felt like my chest cavity was cracking or straightening itself into place. My head and the back of my left shoulder then began to feel lighter. It felt like I had been carrying a heavy load on these areas of my body that was lifting. Then the sensation I had before with my chest and heart resumed.

As I continued to scream, it felt like someone had inserted a pipe between my left breast and heart. I could feel air escaping from what felt like a pipe that was letting out air from my chest while at the same time feeling some strange movement between my left breast and chest. It seemed like I had a thousand pounds of heavy cement laid on my chest at that point.

Those feelings did not come upon me all at once. But things like that happened over the course of many days. My breathing was weak for days, and I had no energy. Then my left leg began to shake frequently as if I had restless leg syndrome. Sometimes it jerked so much that it hurt me terribly.

There was a whole lot more that this body of mine endured during that time, but I am limiting the list of my experiences and giving you a condensed account of what I am calling the beginning of the exodus.

It should be clear at this point that I have not reached the end of my story about God transforming my life since I am still writing about the violent throes of the battle I was fighting before reaching the end of it. And I will tell you more, but let me put the story on *pause* for a moment.

There was not much for me to do or say (or believe) than to conclude that the true Spirit of God was continuing to work at rectifying what sin and disobedience had caused. And for that I am eternally grateful and unapologetic in proclaiming, "Isn't God marvelous?"

But people may ask why I am putting so much effort into providing such a detailed account of my experiences. Well, simply put, being totally transparent about my experiences and writing many of them down is my attempt to build a memorial to stand testimony to the acts and greatness of God. I want my experiences to become like the stones Joshua commanded the Israelites to gather from the bottom of the Jordan River to stack up as a memorial to how God cut off the water of the river to bring them into the promised land.

> *Then Joshua said to the Israelites, "In the future your children will ask, 'What do these stones mean?' Then you can tell them, 'This is where the Israelites crossed the Jordan on dry ground.' For the Lord your God dried up the river right before your eyes, and he kept it dry until you were all across, just as he did at the Red Sea when he dried it up until we had all crossed over. He did this so all the nations of the earth might know that the Lord's hand is powerful, and so you might fear the Lord your God forever."*
> (Joshua 4:21-24 NLT)

And on at least some occasions when Jesus healed and delivered the oppressed, He told them to go and tell others about it. After Jesus delivered the man who was possessed by a legion of demons, the man begged Jesus to let him follow Him, but Jesus told him, *"Return to your own house, and tell what great things God has done for you"* (Luke 8:39a NKJV).

We need to hear the testimonies of those whom the Lord has delivered and set free. And I must proclaim from the house tops if possible what *great things* God has done for *me*. And I could not be satisfied with my effort in testifying to His acts without being as transparent as I have been in my writing. God deserves nothing less from me in my attempt to testify to His faithfulness, power, and glory.

My testimony may not be anything like yours. In fact, perhaps my testimony is also unique among *all* those you have read others relate, but whatever God has done, it is worth sharing for the benefit of others. I encourage you to tell your story of salvation and deliverance to others. Build a memorial. Don't hold back. Then believe God to use your testimony for His purpose to encourage many to come to Him.

As I continue to look back on my life, and especially on the things I and Camilla went through in recent years, it makes me wonder about many things. For instance, had my tormenter been present all along in my life? Or was it attracted to me during the course of my attempts to draw closer to God?

Did I play any role in inviting something other than the Spirit of God to live with me or influence me when I traveled home to Sierra Leone to be with my family? Or when I visited the church campsite when my mother was living with us—was there something about it that became an invitation for such a spiritual attack on me?

Perhaps there was something I allowed by sharing my dreams with a total stranger to gain understanding. And perhaps I invited more trouble by yielding myself to error and false beliefs by following the counsel of spiritual leaders I shouldn't have listened to. Perhaps I allowed too many people who had too many views to pray for us and offer us guidance during our time of need.

Could my enemy have been something I attracted through my own sinful nature? And then for the million-dollar question—what part did ancestral idol worship on the part of my family have to do with it?

No doubt these are all valid questions. But I have come to believe that if I were to spend the rest of my life trying to make sense of every piece of the puzzle, and if I were to seek to uncover every detail of every secret still hidden in the history of my family—if I refused to release to God my need to know every reason for everything, it would mean that I would fail to ever completely trust that Jesus defeated what I can't understand on that fateful day on Calvary so long ago.

And so, victory is present every day despite what the enemy would have wanted me to believe. The Apostle John recorded these words of Jesus:

> *I have told you these things, so that in Me you may have [perfect] peace. In the world, you have tribulation and distress and suffering, but be courageous [be confident, be undaunted, be filled with joy]; I have overcome the world. [My conquest is accomplished, My victory abiding.]* (John 16:33 AMP)

I aim to always adhere to the Master's Words. So while I always want to learn more of what He has to teach me, I am at the same time determined to yield to Him my lack of understanding about the things confronted in this life and live in the peace He gives to us through every situation.

CHAPTER 13

The Exodus

Now the length of time the Israelite people lived in Egypt was 430 years. At the end of the 430 years, to the very day, all the LORD's divisions left Egypt. (Exodus 12:40-41)

THE HOLY SPIRIT had been training me to be sensitive to His voice. And just before Christmas in 2020, I sensed a pulling in my spirit to listen to more of the late Kenneth E. Hagin's messages. I had also been reading some of his books during that period. As I listened, I felt in my heart that I would like to visit the church where he was able to be such a faithful servant.

That church is in Oklahoma, a long drive from Georgia, but I was ready to travel there. However, there was a problem. I had agreed to take my daughter to Virginia. I was in a pickle, but I knew I needed to honor the plans we had already made. With that, I resolved to visit Pastor Hagin's church, Rhema Bible Church, during the first week of the New Year following our return from Virginia.

But it was as if God was honoring what I wanted to do when only one day before we were to leave for Virginia, my daughter said, "I don't want to go to Virginia anymore."

What? I felt guilty because I thought I might have done something or said something to cause her to change her mind. So I asked for her reason for canceling her trip. She said, "I just don't want to go anymore."

Hallelujah! David wrote, *"Take delight in the Lord, and he will give you the desires of your heart"* (Psalm 37:4).

I did not hesitate to start planning our trip to Broken Arrow, Oklahoma—the location of the church. And within two days we began the eight hundred mile (one way) journey. My nine-year-old nephew came along with us. (I call him my nephew, but he's actually my sister-friend's middle child.)

We spent the first night of our trip in a hotel in Memphis. The next day we went out the door at 4:30 AM to continue the rest of our journey to Broken Arrow. We finally arrived there close to noon that day and checked into our hotel. I was excited as I changed my clothes and raced to the Rhema campus in anticipation of walking their grounds. (They also have a college there by the church.)

When I arrived, I sat in the car and looked at the church building where he had preached many messages that had inspired me and drawn me into a deeper understanding of God's Word. My eyes made contact with the distinctive logo that sits in the middle of the church's roof that spells out the word, FAITH.

It was only appropriate that he had the logo displayed so prominently since he was a man of faith and was called to preach faith to God's people. And that he did it with excellence is evident by his legacy.

I had so many mixed emotions going through my head as I sat there. I began to dialogue with God about my desires, which I quietly spoke to His listening ears.

I cannot describe how I felt. I was planning to visit the Rhema Bible Training College campus at some point during our visit there since I had looked into the school when a friend had recommended it. But after arriving at the church, I found myself visiting the school before touring the church since its location was so convenient.

I was nervous and excited at the same time. I felt blessed to walk the grounds that Kenneth Hagin walked. I looked at the buildings, and they all looked as if they had been there since he was alive. Everything looked to be original, which I learned during my visit was true.

After some time had passed, I then went into one of the college buildings where classes are held to meet with the admissions staff. I wanted to explore attending the school. But I just missed the person I needed to see by minutes because she had gone to lunch. A staff member asked me to return in an hour. I said, "Thank you," but instead of leaving I decided to stay on the grounds until the admissions official returned and use the opportunity to visit the church and give myself a more thorough tour of the campus.

I left the building I was in and walked around to the main church building as I marveled at its simplicity. But while it looked less fancy, or less impressive than so many megachurches these days, God's wondrous works have been and are still being displayed there. Then I began wondering to myself why more miracles are not being seen in more of our churches today. "What could be wrong?" I wondered.

And I ask you, how could those men and women of old— some being called "God's Generals" by some—yield to the power of the Holy Spirit and perform such miraculous works, but so many spiritual leaders today can't? God raised the dead through Smith Wigglesworth. He caused the lame to walk through Oral Roberts. He opened the eyes of the blind and caused the deaf to hear through Kathryn Kuhlman and drove out demons through Kenneth Hagin.[22]

This is merely a brief list of many mighty miracles God performed through people of faith in the not-so-distant past. How could they have displayed such power to do the work of God's kingdom being they were just as ordinary as many men and women of God I have come to know today?

As I thought about that question, it dawned on me that they were not just called by God; they were obedient to the call by actually doing what God wanted them to do. They did not make themselves what they became. It was God who made them what they were. Nor did they seek to take the glory for what God's spirit did through them.

They had the fear of God in them. They did not seek to serve their own interests or make a name for themselves. Rather, they surrendered to the leading of the Holy Spirit with a reverence for God's mandate. They devoted time to studying the Word of God by sacrificing their pride and dying to self in the secret place. They understood the cost our Savior had to pay in order for them to gain such a privilege to be called faithful co-heirs of Christ.

Moreover, they were not bothered by not having all of the finest things in life. Their focus was to serve God under the circumstances in which they lived. And even though in time many

---

22 Although Kenneth Hagin was called to preach faith, he also had a well-known healing and deliverance ministry.

of them ended up preaching in large arenas and fancy buildings, they showed that they didn't need those before they could preach the Good News.

The late Reinhard Bonnke is an example of such a faithful preacher. He was a beloved servant of God who displayed genuine humility when God called for his life and led him to leave what was familiar to pick up his cross and travel the extents of Africa for the sake of the Gospel.

If you do not know the stories and ministries behind such great servants of God, I suggest you ask God to lead you in becoming familiar with such a generation of pioneers of the Gospel.

What they had is what so many churches and church leaders are missing today. But what God did through those I mentioned here, He can still do through committed believers today, because the power and goals of the Holy Spirit never change!

These thoughts played in my head as I walked through the door into the church and began pacing through the hallway. I could feel a pulling in my spirit that I cannot adequately describe. I tried to enter the church's sanctuary, but the doors were locked. Regardless, though, I was being blessed by being there.

I then left the church and made my way to another building named *The Praying and Healing Center.* I was eager to go in and sit where Pastor Hagin taught and get a sense of the miraculous healings that took place from there. But I was not able to go in because prayer meetings were being held. However, I was able to look inside and spoke with someone who personally knew Brother Hagin and his wife, who is also now gone.

What a joy to hear firsthand of his humility and his heart for God's people. I talked with that person for a while before I said my goodbyes. I then returned to the Bible School building to meet with the admissions staff.

When I made my way back there, the person I was supposed to talk to was not at her desk. I felt a prompting to leave, but I refused to leave because I thought if I left before the person came back I would be missing out on something. So again I stayed on the campus.

I walked around the building and admired the classrooms—how they were set up, and how large they were. All around inside the building, I could not help but notice that the furniture and decorations looked to be the originals. That had a certain appeal to me. All the while, I continued to talk with God quietly.

Spending time on the campus actually became my routine for the next five days while I was in Broken Arrow, and during that time, I considered the campus to be my secret place.

I felt a bit tired from my drive at some point, so I sat down in one corner of the lobby of the building with my head on my legs and dozed off for a few minutes. I set my alarm to wake me up at 1:30 PM, because by that time I had gotten an email message from the admissions staff to meet then. But I woke up before my alarm went off.

I finally made my way to the official's office and sat directly in front of her as we spoke. I asked about her time at the school, to which she responded and gave me a bit of her history. She also shared things with me about Pastor Hagin and his wife, and what she said confirmed what I had sensed from his preaching and teachings and from what the other staff from the Healing School had already shared with me.

The Bible says, *"By the mouth of two or three witnesses every word shall be established"* (2 Corinthians 13:1b NKJV). The school's staff members validated what I had concluded about the man of God and my desire to visit his church community. However, I still felt there was more to my visit than simply confirming my conclusion of his character and exploring the thought of attending the school.

Suddenly, the official said, "I am going to give you a tour."

We walked out through the double doors and headed straight for the church building. I shared with her that I had been in the church earlier and bought some books from the bookstore. She continued to lead me across the parking lot and into the church. Then using keys in her hand, she unlocked one of the sanctuary's doors. She motioned for me to walk ahead of her, and we entered the sanctuary.

I only have one word to describe what I saw, "Breathtaking!" Some who know the building may disagree with me because of how it might compare to huge, fancy churches they've attended. However, as they say, beauty is in the eye of the beholder.

The entire interior of the church has been remodeled and transformed with a gray and brownish palette of colors. It was very inviting to me. And I sensed being there in that place was perhaps more important to me than it was to many others on a tour of a facility It was increasingly feeling like a divine appointment.

As the admissions official talked about the church and what they had done, all I wanted was to put my hands on the altar. My mind was consumed with thoughts that filled my mind with wonder, amazement, hunger, and desire.

I interrupted and said, "Can I place my hand on the altar?"

She said, "Of course."

I walked down in front of the platform and placed my right hand on the altar thanking God for such a tremendous opportunity. Then, without me asking, the official placed her right hand next to mine to agree with me without knowing what was in my heart. We both began to thank God for some minutes.

After a few minutes in prayer, we left the altar area and started to walk out of the sanctuary. But as we walked away I heard in my spirit that I had not placed my left hand on the altar. So I stopped dead in my tracks, walked toward the altar on the other side of the sanctuary, put my left hand on the altar, and thanked God again.

The admissions official stood in the middle of the room and watched me. Overwhelmed with gratitude, I then joined her, and we walked out of the sanctuary. As we made our way out of the building, suddenly a gust of wind blew so hard that I thought both the official and I would be carried away. Then my left hand started shaking so violently that I thought it would separate from my body.

All I could say was, "Whoa, whoa!," as we walked across back to her office.

Of course, having experienced so many other physical manifestations, I knew that was no coincidence. But I left the matter between God and me and never discussed it with my guide. She did not comment on it either, perhaps chucking it up to nature. For me, though, I sighed within myself, "The deep things of God."

Based on my conversation with the official, there were several church services scheduled as well as other campus events, because it was during the holidays. I decided to participate in some of them with my daughter and my nephew. And that seemed natural since I had already decided to form a schedule of walking the grounds daily to pray and worship God.

As I said earlier when I decided to stay on campus after learning the admissions official was not available, if I didn't follow through with that, "I would be missing out on something." If you are questioning my seemingly endless or tireless pursuit of things—that it seems somewhat over the top, so to speak (and that as you might have considered was also expensive)—tell me this:

How many people idealize those in the entertainment industry, sports, or even in politics? How adamant are they in *their* pursuits? How much time and money do *they* spend going to their favorite events all over the country?

For me, the things of God are my rush. And considering the men and women of God whose work has yielded such meaningful results for God's Kingdom—from whom I have come to learn of God and spiritual matters, and to whom I have come to feel connected—I am not ashamed to say that I have a burning desire to know more about their work and draw closer to the God they served.

And I get excited even walking on the paths where they walked, seeing an old house where they grew up, or standing in the buildings where they preached. So yes, that was a routine I was going to adhere to.

Around noon every day, the children and I left the hotel and drove to the campus. We walked over the entire grounds. Following that, we sat in the car each day and worshiped.

I could tell my daughter was getting a little impatient with the repetitive schedule. It probably took her mind back to our painful seven day adventure that had shaken her to the core. And I knew it must be strange in the eyes of a teenager that her mother would take her on an eight-hundred mile trip during Christmas week for such an adventure.

Of course she was more than a little familiar with many strange things that affected my life, and hence, hers as well. Clearly, though, only she and God knew her thoughts. And she wasn't verbally complaining to me (she is definitely a patient soul). But I could see that she wasn't understanding it all, so without her asking, I took the opportunity to explain myself.

One of the blessings of having Camilla as my daughter is that she is sensitive to the things of God. So she does not argue with me but simply agrees to accept things once she understands what is being done. The Bible says, *"Direct your children onto the right path, and when they are older, they will not leave it"* (Proverbs 22:6 NLT).

One day as we were going to the Rhema campus from the hotel, I began to feel in my spirit that I should visit the late Oral Roberts' campus (Oral Roberts University in Tulsa, just west of Rhema Bible Training College in Broken Arrow). I said, "Lord, I didn't come here to go to Oral Robert's place." But that feeling didn't leave me.

As we sat in the hotel room later that evening, I was on my bed, and my daughter and nephew were sitting on the other bed occupying themselves with their electronic devices. Unexpectedly, my daughter said, "We should go to Tulsa." She continued, "I checked; it's only seventeen minutes away from where we are now."

And here's what will jerk you from your seat. I had just been on my phone looking up Oral Roberts' ministries and saw the location of their campus was only a twenty minutes' drive from our hotel.

Up until then, the idea of visiting the Oral Roberts campus had simply been in my spirit. so I just decided to read and learn more about the campus. I hadn't said anything to Camilla about it. But after what she said, I felt I had a confirmation that I should go, so we decided to visit the campus on the upcoming Saturday.

That conversation with Camilla happened on Thursday, Christmas Eve of 2020. We got up early on the following Saturday and had our normal morning prayer and worship time (It doesn't matter whether we are on vacation or not; we keep to this routine.) Then we were out through the door headed for Tulsa.

During my visit to Oral Roberts University, I didn't have so many thoughts or emotions as I had experienced while visiting the Rhema campus. Nevertheless, prior to our visit I had been listening for a few months to the late Oral Roberts' preaching and teachings recorded during his healing services. His passion for God's people is evident to see during his services. So I was not wholly surprised by the pull I felt to visit the site where he established the campus.

During my research of his campus, I had seen pictures of the Praying Hands monument and the Healing Tower on the campus grounds. With all I had learned, my interest was especially drawn to the monument of the Praying Hands. So upon our arrival, that was the first thing I wanted to see.

As we made our way around the parking lots, I set my eyes on finding the Praying Hands statue. We soon found it, and I was immediately overcome with emotions. My whole body was shaking, but not from being cold. I began to cry with a heart of gratitude that I had been found worthy to see a piece of history that symbolizes the miraculous work of the Holy Spirit through the divine healing ministry of an ordinary man.

I shared earlier about thinking I knew God based on what my relationship had been with Him up until that point. In all actuality,

I have come to realize I knew only a small fraction about Him and His works. I have apologized to God for having been so slow to learn there are levels of understanding God and His ways that I hadn't even begun to tap into.

But isn't He faithful? Isn't He patient to allow us to journey as long as many of us have with such limited knowledge of Him while believing we knew Him as well as we needed to? I am overwhelmed with God's ability to love us as we are and His willingness to draw us closer to Him with baby foods until we reach some level of maturity when He can begin feeding us solid nourishment.[23]

As I continued to learn more of Him, I began to understand why He intended to send us the Holy Spirit. The Holy Spirit is clearly the *Mighty Helper,* and it is only through His infinite power that we are allowed the ability to connect with God in a way that isn't possible otherwise.

Can you feel my excitement as I write about these divine relationships? I hope something will stir in your spirit to give *you* such excitement!

I stepped out of the car and walked up to that massive monument showing a portion of two forearms with two big hands drawn together in a praying posture. The monument weighs thirty tons and stands sixty feet tall, and it is one of the largest bronze sculptures in the world.

---

23 "We have much to say about this, but it is hard to make it clear to you because you no longer try to understand. In fact, though by this time you ought to be teachers, you need someone to teach you the elementary truths of God's word all over again. You need milk, not solid food! Anyone who lives on milk, being still an infant, is not acquainted with the teaching about righteousness. But solid food is for the mature, who by constant use have trained themselves to distinguish good from evil" (Hebrews 5:11-14).

My daughter and nephew were taking pictures as they, too, marveled at its beauty. As I pressed myself against the base of the monument, I silently prayed to God, "Heart to heart, Father to daughter." My daughter and nephew then joined me as they also leaned into the monument and prayed their secret prayers to God.

As I approached the side of the monument closest to me after arriving, I saw an inscription on the granite base. It boldly proclaims:

"...Death is swallowed up in victory."

1 Corinthians 15:54 (KJV)

Then I walked around the entire monument with both of my hands touching its entire circumference as I continued to pray. I then stood in front of the monument and read the inscription engraved on that side:

"And Jesus grew in wisdom and stature, and in favor with God and man"   **Luke 2:52**

Luke 2:52 is very appropriate for engraving on a monument that stands in front of an educational institution dedicated to preparing students for representing their creator in many callings and occupations around the world.

Paul told Timothy:

Study and do your best to present yourself to God approved, a workman [tested by trial] who has no reason to be ashamed, accurately handling and skillfully teaching the word of truth.

(2 Timothy 2:15 AMP)

I have heard well-known preachers say that Oral Roberts was "a man of prayer." And after becoming acquainted with Brother Roberts' preaching and ministry, I feel he must have also been a studious man of God's Word.

Directly behind from where I was standing, there were three individual plates with inscriptions on them. The one in the middle showed Oral Roberts, and written on it was his testimony of what he said was a direct command from God to build the university. I placed both of my hands on that plate and prayed.

After spending time at the Praying Hands sculpture, we proceeded to walk toward the core of the university and into what looked like a garden or small park. There were Christmas lights, trees, and decorative items everywhere. And the atmosphere of that place could easily become one's secret place to commune with God in stillness.

We made our way into the garden, where we found the statue of Jesus as the *Master Teacher.* It consisted of Jesus sitting with two individuals sitting before Him, a man and a woman, as He taught them. The children took pictures there as well.

I then decided to go see something else that caught my eye as we walked. It was an old tree that had been carved into the image of Jesus. It stood still there alone and looked as old as it can be. The children and I looked at it attentively. Then they walked ahead of me while I continued to admire the craftsmanship and talents of God's people. I considered how the ability to do such artwork could only come from the Divine Master himself.

As I walked down the path to meet the children, I heard these words spoken to me, "Pray. Pray always."

There was no one there besides the children and me. The voice was deep and that of a man. I looked behind me and smiled. Then I said, "Yes Lord."

Isaiah wrote:

Your own ears will hear him. Right behind you a voice will say, "This is the way you should go, whether to the right or to the left." (Isaiah 30:21 NLT)

And David wrote:

The LORD says, "I will guide you along the best pathway for your life. I will advise you and watch over you." (Psalm 32:8 NLT)

I had come to understand that God can speak to us in many ways, even verbally if He chooses. The Bible records the truth of that. So if God speaks to you, you are in good company.

Having heard the command to *pray*, and *pray always*, I concluded that it was time for me to return my focus to the main reason I traveled to Oklahoma. The children and I then left and headed out to dinner.

As the evening went on, I reflected on everything that had happened so far on the trip and was thankful for all of them. That Christmas, like so many others in my life, I didn't receive a material gift, but I received something more profound that no amount of money can buy. I felt blessed!

Back at the hotel, we prayed and thanked God for the day. Then I lay down on the bed. But sleeping became a challenge. The enemy was determined to bring me misery. As I tried to fall asleep, I began to see imagery of places and people playing right in front of my eyes. I attempted to ignore it, but it continued. Then I saw before me the trick of the imagery of snakes. I did my best to ignore that too.

Many attempts were made to confuse and discourage me as those images continued to be displayed in front of me—even with my eyes closed. I prayed and made declarations. However, the many displays continued to appear, so I got up and turned on a recording of a message by one of the men of God I mentioned to you and let it play all night.

I had already learned from Scripture that God has not given us a spirit of fear, and I rested in that.

For God did not give us a spirit of timidity or cowardice or fear, but [He has given us a spirit] of power and love and of sound judgment and personal discipline [abilities that result in a calm, well-balanced mind and self-control]. (2 Timothy 1:7 AMP)

As I lay there that night, I decided again to stand on the word and proclaim, "He who is in me is greater than he that's in the world."[24]

We got up in the morning and got ready for church. It was the last Sunday of the year 2020. I was excited to be in the house of the Lord again to prove to the enemy that nothing would keep me from the house of God and from giving my attention to all things pertaining to His kingdom.

I had been praying to receive the genuine gift of the indwelling of the Holy Spirit with the evidence of speaking in tongues—God's way. My prayer had been for the pastor to lay hands on us while at church to receive the baptism. However, I didn't know any of the people to approach the pastor on my behalf. So I said, "Lord, you know how to orchestrate all things. you could speak to the pastor who preaches to do an altar call so we can receive the gift of the Holy Spirit."

If that didn't happen like I asked, I also thought I would find a way to approach the pastor to make my request. I assumed the minister preaching in the Sunday service would be the late Rev.

---

24 "You, dear children, are from God and have overcome them, because the one who is in you is greater than the one who is in the world" (1 John 4:4).

Hagin's son or his wife, who had preached on Christmas Eve. But as it turned out, the preacher that day was Kenneth Hagin's grandson. He was the same young man I had seen in many of his grandfather's videos.

He made an altar call toward the end of the service. And for several minutes he encouraged people in need of salvation or those in need of rededication to come forward. Then to my joy, he said, "If you desire the gift of the indwelling of the Holy Spirit to speak in tongues, come forward."

I grabbed my daughter and nephew and raced to the front. We stood in front of the altar—the very same altar where I had laid my hands a few days earlier and prayed. I thought, "How faithful is our God!"

He prayed over us, and we were then escorted to a room where we were prayed for again. As the pastor prayed for me there in that room, I let out some loud sounds and began feeling very cold as my body shook. I received by faith what God had promised, and the Holy Spirit filled me. Both my daughter and nephew were with me. And I believe God also bestowed the precious gift of the Holy Spirit in them as well.

We left church with educational materials to help us continue our spiritual growth. And then we spent some time driving around the city until evening before returning to the hotel to prepare to head back to Georgia first thing the next morning, which we did at 4:00 AM.

As you can imagine, we were all exhausted but refreshed spiritually. I felt charged up and ready to continue my pursuit of the things of God.

God called Moses to go before Pharaoh and tell him God demanded that he let His people leave Egypt. Pharaoh refused God's directions several times, but God's demand was finally met. And it was a day of victory when the Children of Israel followed Moses into the desert toward the promised land. It was a day of rejoicing when the people exited the land where they had so long been in bondage.

As God's representative, Moses stood in the gap for the Children of Israel, and they were delivered by God's hand.

I have known bondage. I have known the abuse that God's enemies can lay upon God's people. But I have also learned that God's people are never alone in the land of their bondage. And God is still calling men and women who, like Moses, will answer God's call to deliver His people.

God knows what His people are going through. He is mindful of their suffering. And He is always working in the midst of it all. He is even using the things that cause them suffering and pain to prepare them for their own exodus from oppression and affliction.

And even after their exodus, with every step they take through what can indeed become a desert of challenges, they are—like faithful Joshua—being prepared by God to stride into the promised land with confidence to conquer all those who stand in defiance against God and His people.

CHAPTER 14

Strengthen Your Brethren

And the Lord said, "Simon, Simon! Indeed, Satan has [desired to have you,] [25] *that he may sift you as wheat. But I have prayed for you, that your faith should not fail; and when you have returned to Me, strengthen your brethren."* (Luke 22:31-32 NKJV)

JESUS WAS ON the shore of the Sea of Galilee one day surrounded by people who were interested in his teachings. He entered into a boat belonging to a man named Simon, who later became almost universally known as Peter. [26]

25 "Desired to have you" is the wording of the King James Version.
26 Simon Peter had earlier been introduced to Jesus by Andrew, Peter's brother (John 1:40-41). It was at that earlier meeting when Jesus told Simon, *"You are Simon the son of Jonah. You shall be called Cephas" (which is translated, A Stone)"* (John 1:42b NKJV). "Cephas" is Aramaic for stone or rock (neither a big rock or small rock, merely rock), and "Peter" is Greek for rock.

Jesus asked Peter to put out from the shore a little, where Jesus continued to teach the people from the boat. And *"when he had finished speaking, he said to Simon, 'Put out into deep water, and let down your nets for a catch'"* (Luke 5:4).

Simon answered, "Master, we've worked hard all night and haven't caught anything. But because you say so, I will let down the nets."

When they had done so, they caught such a large number of fish that their nets began to break. So they signaled their partners in the other boat to come and help them, and they came and filled both boats so full that they began to sink.

When Simon Peter saw this, he fell at Jesus' knees and said, "Go away from me, Lord; I am a sinful man!" For he and all his companions were astonished at the catch of fish they had taken, and so were James and John, the sons of Zebedee, Simon's partners.

Then Jesus said to Simon, "Don't be afraid; from now on you will fish for people." So they pulled their boats up on shore, left everything and followed him. (Luke 5:5-11)

After that experience, Simon's life was never the same as he was launched into a new life and vocation. From reading Scripture we see that Simon Peter was strong willed and determined. And just as he was determined to be the best fisherman he could be, Peter became determined to be a faithful follower of Jesus.

And by the time we get to the twenty-second chapter of Luke and read what Jesus told him, it's clear that the enemy knew Peter's value to the work of the Gospel and eyed him for destruction.

I'm convinced that anytime people answer God's call and decide to follow Him, there will be those moments or circumstances when they are faced with temptation and experiences that could cause them to stumble. Peter definitely found that true when under pressure he denied Christ.[27]

I had decided to follow God long ago, but as you have read in this book, I had a long way to go before I was going to be able to follow Him in knowledge and wisdom. But I knew God had a plan for my life, and I was determined to find it. And just as Peter had to experience failure and dejection before he could one day stand before the multitudes on the Day of Pentecost and proclaim God's Word to them, I have experienced many things.

Satan wanted to sift Peter like wheat, and I feel like the enemy has been sifting me for years. But Jesus knew all about it, and I have come to expect Jesus to bring something out of it all for my good, my daughter's good, and for the good of many others. He did that for Peter, and in His grace, I believe He will do that for me.

Jesus is not only the *author* of our faith but also the *finisher* (Hebrews 12:2 NKJV). And we have the assurance that He is our *"ever-present help in trouble"* (Psalm 46:1).

Jesus, who foreknows everything about our lives, stands in the gap between His children and the stumbling blocks that try to overtake us—even stumbling blocks we do not see or even realize exist. Through the power of the Holy Spirit, He intercedes for us so the enemy's attempts to destroy our lives are thwarted.

But beyond that, I believe Jesus calls out to everyone who responds to Him in faith and speaks the same words He spoke to Peter: *"Strengthen your brethren."*

---

27 "Peter replied, 'Man, I don't know what you're talking about!' Just as he was speaking, the rooster crowed. The Lord turned and looked straight at Peter. Then Peter remembered the word the Lord had spoken to him: 'Before the rooster crows today, you will disown me three times.' And he went outside and wept bitterly" (Luke 22:60-62).

We are God's children—Christians, people of the faith—and Jesus has given us the victory. He equips us with the Holy Spirit. But He does that for more than our own benefit. We are not only commissioned to adhere to His ways (the Bible way) in obedience and walk in His Light for our own benefit, we are also commissioned to take His Light to others and teach them His ways—to bring people to Jesus and then strengthen them along with other believers.

My daughter and I have learned that the enemy is both persistent and strong to deceive. But we have also learned that we as believers will overcome him by the Blood of the Lamb and the word of our testimony (Revelation 12:11). And in many ways, that is the central message we can offer to others to strengthen them.

Although I claimed faith and wanted to both know and serve God faithfully, I know now that I was not successful in those things for a long time because I didn't have a firm foundation on which to build my spiritual house. I had not received proper teaching. And no one in my family provided to me a proper example to follow.

Not having a firm footing or a map to follow then, my understanding was darkened, and thus I continued down the wrong path—even while I determined to know and live for God. Nonetheless, through many mistakes, His sovereignty and patience kept me from self-destruction. And over time, my wonderful Lord kept pouring out His grace to me, and step by step He led me out of error into His truth.

Instead of the adult leaders of my family faithfully serving God and leading me into the paths of righteousness (the way it is supposed to work), they made decisions that both fostered confusion and invited forces of darkness to have power not only over the family at large but also individual members of it—members like me.

From my childhood—before I could make any informed decisions of my own—the enemy was already placing a claim on my life. From my childhood I was involved in a spiritual battle.

My testimony is unlike those of vast numbers of people. But I know I'm not the only one who has suffered because people have attempted to be a Christian while at the same time being bound by idolatrous beliefs and occult practices. There are many who still today readily accept Christianity but refuse to let go of their devilish beliefs. They are like the Athenians to whom Paul preached about *The Unknown God.*

The Athenians were very *religious,* and they had all sorts of gods. They built edifices and altars to them. And to make sure they didn't miss a god that they had yet to learn about, they built an altar with the inscription *"TO AN UNKNOWN GOD"* (Acts 17:23).

Basically, the Athenians were more than ready and willing to accept another god. But not so many of them were willing to serve only the God Paul went to Athens to present to them. I have come to accept and devote my life to the Only True God, and I reject all others. I will serve no others, and I will continue to warn others to divorce themselves from all occult practices and idolatry of all forms.

But clearly, I had and still have family members who have not made the same decision.

To all too many people, Christianity is simply another religion instead of a way of life. But Christianity is based on and only exists through a personal relationship with the Father. And that relationship was purchased for us only through the precious Blood of Jesus.

People who attempt to be a Christian while still serving other gods or holding non-Christian, unbiblical philosophies are fooling themselves. All beliefs contrary to what the Bible reveals to us about pleasing God and living for Him must be rejected, and the Bible reveals to us the extent to which that must be done.

> *Be careful to do everything I have said to you. Do not invoke the names of other gods; do not let them be heard on your lips.*
> (Exodus 23:13)

> *Do not worship any other god, for the LORD, whose name is Jealous, is a jealous God.* (Exodus 34:14)

> *Jesus is "the stone you builders rejected, which has become the cornerstone." Salvation is found in no one else, for there is no other name under heaven given to mankind by which we must be saved.* (Acts 4:11-12)

While acknowledging a belief in God, and while laying claim to Christianity, the devotion of all too many consists only of attending church services, paying tithes and offerings, and perhaps performing other works that are intended to show they accept the dogma of religion. But all of that actually becomes meaningless if their lives deny their overwhelming need to actually know and follow God—have knowledge and understanding of what is written in the Book of Life, and then act on it.

I have written much about my struggles to break free of the influences of what the secrets of my family had left to me in the way of a spiritual inheritance—a very negative inheritance. But while multitudes will never know what it is like to have to emerge from the effects of such spiritual darkness as I have known, there are perhaps even more who are bound by other things they inherited.

So many young people today face the effects of parents imparting to them a fractured life dependent on their love of possessions and wanton lifestyles. And all it takes is a look around us to see how so many believers, and even so many churches, are bound by their pursuit of the world instead of their pursuit of God.

The Gospel of the Cross that was once preached from so many pulpits has been replaced by feel-good and prosperity messages. And churches full of people are not only accepting but reveling in following the gods of the world without even realizing it.

How has the Body of Christ become so focused on respecting the wishes and desires of men and women versus the wishes and desires—and in fact the mandates—of God? What will it take to understand that much of what we see today in our societies are the operations of the enemy at work? How do we explain the many types of sicknesses, violence, poverty, and discord and strife in our governments, families, and in so many other areas?

It's time for that to change. And it's past time for the Church to turn back to its roots.

During my studying, and through my personal experiences, I have seen that the African churches have allocated a vast part of their ministries to "spiritual warfare." And clearly there is a need for such ministries. However, in their well doing I think rather than elevating the power of the Holy Spirit's ministry, they have too often aggrandized the works of the enemy.

I get it that satanic practices are prone to be prominent in the African nations. And I have learned from personal experiences that the trouble and long-lasting results of such practices are very, very real. But I have come to believe there needs to be a better balance between the warfare we declare we must do and the resting we must do in what Jesus has already done.

We know Jesus has already defeated the enemy and put all powers and authorities under His feet.

And having disarmed the powers and authorities, he made a public spectacle of them, triumphing over them by the cross.
(Colossians 2:15)

Part of our duties as Christ's followers is to simply be vessels He can work through to heal the sick and speak deliverance to the captives. And we proclaim the truth of Colossians 2:15 as we go about doing it. Certainly we are to pray and proclaim, and that can be done in a fairly animated way, but there is rest and peace in knowing that the battle is ultimately the Lord's. And that fosters balance in our lives.

Winning spiritual battles is not dependent on our power. It is dependent on Jesus. And as we invite His involvement into our lives, our faith and trust in Him releases His power to work in us.

Especially during the period of time I covered in this book, my mind was largely on my own spiritual needs as well as on the needs of my daughter. And I spent days, weeks, months, and yes, years, seeking strength and help from others to have our needs met.

I looked to a dream interpreter I should not have even spoken to. I looked to spiritual leaders who sometimes helped me but sometimes led me in the wrong direction. And I looked to friends. But fortunately I kept pressing to know the Word of God and found what I ultimately needed in the arms and wisdom of God.

All of those experiences will always be part of my memory and building blocks in my life. But now my focus has turned to the burning desire I have to strengthen the brethren—people like you—to strengthen your resolve to draw close to God and never end your pursuit of the Truth.

So I speak a declaration over you that Paul wrote to the believers in Ephesus.

> *I pray that out of his glorious riches he may strengthen you with power through his Spirit in your inner being, so that Christ may dwell in your hearts through faith. And I pray that you, being rooted and established in love, may have power, together with all the Lord's holy people, to grasp how wide and long and high and deep is the love of Christ, and to know this love that surpasses knowledge—that you may be filled to the measure of all the fullness of God."* (Ephesians 3:16-19)

Amen!

EPILOGUE

I LAID OUT my truth in the pages of this book in hopes of helping anyone who can benefit from it. I held nothing back, because I believe my willingness to make myself vulnerable to you is central in my effort to reveal the depth of God's desire to transform lives—no matter how confused and broken they may appear.

It was through the process of God transforming my life that I believe I finally discovered the reason for which I was born. And true, spiritual transformation will surely bear similar results in others. And that's because when we're transformed we discover God made us to not merely know *of* Him, to not merely pray *to* Him, and to not merely believe *in* Him, but to have a loving, close, and powerful personal relationship *with* Him.

That changes everything!

It definitely changed me. So now, like one of the five smart virgins who carried extra oil for their lamps as they journeyed to meet the bridegroom (Matthew 25:1-13), I have determined to always maintain extra jars of oil by staying connected to the Holy Spirit's work in me. I want to ensure my lamp will be burning at all times in anticipation of meeting the Church's Bridegroom, Jesus.

And more than ever, I desire to be the mother my daughter needs. And with the Holy Spirit's help, I am determined to continue to be in her life when I am needed and offer to her the things God has taught me through my life's experiences. But my transformation has led me beyond just a concern for those close to me. I want God to use me to bring transformation to the lives of others far beyond the limits of my own family

As I write the ending to this part of my life's story, I am now living in Oklahoma. Yes, my daughter and I have moved once again. But this time there is an entirely different purpose for the move. We moved to Broken Arrow to allow me to attend Bible school. I enrolled in classes at Rhema Bible Training College in Broken Arrow. I am working toward entry into their Itinerant Ministry program. And Lord willing, I hope to also take classes with a focus on world missions.

I'm not certain where this training will lead me in the next chapter of my life, but I am joyfully and confidently committing that to the Lord. I've been changed—transformed—by both God's love and His patience with me, and I'm determined to be a yielded vessel for Christ and let Him determine how to use me.

Days before my decision to attend Bible school, I read the book of Second Timothy. Paul's words to Timothy inspired me, and after reading it, I concluded that the Lord has great expectations for me. And with the help of God's mighty power that dwells in me, I have no intention of failing Him! I pray that you will also seek to know and fulfil His expectations for *you*.

And as you and I both draw closer to God and seek to follow Him to do whatever He calls us to do, let us always value the lives of those who are seemingly lost without hope. God loves the people we see who seem to live in constant confusion, drama, and turmoil. He reaches out to those struggling with spiritual darkness and have trouble breaking free of chains that have long held them bound.

There is amazing hope for them. There is a God in heaven who is not only mindful of their struggle and pain but who also has the solution for them. Our precious Savior died for them. He paid the price for not only their sins but for the complete transformation of their lives. And we need to make sure they discover that.

If they determine to be free—to leave the lowly existence they have known for so long—and allow God to do for them what He has always wanted to do, they will be transformed. They too will allow themselves to be wrapped tightly in the cocoon of God's love. They too will be changed and have their lives restructured. They too will stop crawling on their spiritual belly and learn to soar into the sky as they emerge to new life.

For I am convinced [and continue to be convinced—beyond any doubt] that neither death, nor life, nor angels, nor principalities, nor things present and threatening, nor things to come, nor powers, nor height, nor depth, nor any other created thing, will be able to separate us from the [unlimited] love of God, which is in Christ Jesus our Lord. (Romans 8:38-39 AMP)

CLOSING PRAYERS

A prayer that reflects my greatest desire:

I just want to obey all you ask of me. So teach me, Lord, for you are my God. Your gracious Spirit is all I need, so lead me on good paths that are pleasing to you, my one and only God!

(Psalm 143:10 TPT)

Would you like to pray too?

If you do not have a saving relationship with Jesus, I hope you will now pray the following salvation prayer. And when you do, be sure to sign and date your commitment in the spaces provided and keep it to remind you of your confession of faith.

. . . If you confess with your mouth the Lord Jesus and believe in your heart that God has raised Him from the dead, you will be saved. For with the heart one believes unto righteousness, and with the mouth confession is made unto salvation.

(Romans 10:9-10 NKJV)

The Salvation Prayer:

Dear Lord:

Your Word says, if I declare and confess the Lord Jesus and believe in my heart that God has raised Jesus from the dead, I will be saved. Heavenly Father, I believe with my heart and confess with my mouth that you sent your only begotten Son, Jesus, to die for my salvation. And by His death, burial, resurrection, and ascension into heaven, He has granted me the free gift of salvation, which I now receive. Thus, I am saved.

Thank you, God.

Signed _____

Date _____